The Saint and The Drunk

The Saint and The Drunk

A Guide to Making the Big Decisions in Your Life

By Stephanie Peirolo

SHEPHEARD-WALWYN (PUBLISHERS) LTD

First published in 2025 by
Shepheard-Walwyn (Publishers) Ltd
Suite 108. 4 Little Portland Street London W1W 7JB

www.shepheardwalwyn.com
www.ethicaleconomicbooks.com

British Library Cataloguing in Publication Data
A catalogue record of this book is available from the British Library

paperback ISBN 978-1-916517-11-0
ebook ISBN 978-1-916517-12-7

Typeset by RefineCatch Limited, Bungay, Suffolk

Printed and bound by 4edge Limited

This book is dedicated to the memory of my father, Edward Peirolo,
who taught me about work, the Jesuits, and so much more.

Table of Contents

Introduction

What if we have the capacity to know what is best for us? What if we could access, inside ourselves, a map for our lives that would provide direction at every turning point? What if those directions could be untangled from cultural and familial narratives that don't support us, or tell us we can't do something? What if we could reconnect to moments of knowing with the confidence that we are probably right, and our dreams, hopes and visions for ourselves might be an accurate guide to how we should move forward?

The idea for this book arrived in 2012 when I was working at a small creative advertising agency in Seattle. The office was built like a series of stage sets; the creative department was a putt-putt golf course, the reception area looked like a restaurant with red banquette seats and rubber chickens hung from the front windows. I was in the conference room that was all white. A white grand piano stood on a white shag carpet. We sat around the grand piano's closed top as if it were a conference table. A wall of windows looked out onto the street, which was topped by the Monorail track about two stories up, a souvenir of the 1962 World's Fair.

Danielle was taking my picture. She worked at the agency as a producer as her day job, but she was a photographer. She was taking pictures of me for a business head shot. She told me she wanted to be a photographer full-time and yet wasn't sure if that was the right choice for her to make.

I asked her how she made decisions. Did she do a list of pros and cons? Did she approach it intellectually? Or did she tune into her intuition and other ways of knowing?

She looked at me blankly.

"What do you mean? How do you do that?"

I suggested that she imagine herself in a particular situation. "Picture yourself as a full-time photographer," I said. "Imagine your day in detail. Check in with how you feel about it, being mindful about what you are drawn to or what you resist. Try to get into your body and see what clues your body is giving you."

She was interested. "Where did you learn this? Why haven't you ever talked about this before?"

I paused. "It's from a saint. St. Ignatius of Loyola. He lived in the Middle Ages and came up with a way of making decisions that is called discernment. That became the basis of a process called the Spiritual Exercises of St Ignatius of Loyola. Which I've done. But I feel diffident talking about spiritual practices at work."

Danielle found it helpful, and she didn't find the spiritual component off-putting. She's a tall woman and I remember her putting her camera on one hip and looking at me seriously from across the white room.

"You should write a book about this," she told me.

This book

The intent of this book is to use some of the framework of the Spiritual Exercises of St. Ignatius of Loyola as a foundation for a process to make intentional decisions about work, career or other major life choices. By intentional, I mean that you use your own values, ethics and beliefs to guide you. St. Ignatius of Loyola is the Saint. He was a Catholic priest who founded the Society of Jesus, also known as the Jesuits.

The Exercises, as they are often called, are familiar to many Catholics and there are excellent organizations which can take Catholics or other Christians through the Exercises. I went through them when I was in my thirties, and found it to be a fantastic framework for making decisions, or "discernment" as the Jesuits say.

But when I tried to explain these concepts to friends who were not Catholic, or not religious, I felt the same tension I experienced with Danielle. I wanted to respect their beliefs and hesitated to refer to a process written by a Catholic priest in the Middle Ages that focuses on Jesus and biblical texts.

In 2016 I became an executive coach and found that many of my clients were in a discernment process about work. I wanted to introduce these principles to them, but I kept getting stuck on the God thing. It was, ironically, another spiritual tradition which provided the key to unlock the Exercises for people with a variety of beliefs.

Bill Wilson, the Drunk, co-founded Alcoholics Anonymous. He wrote most if not all of the group's primary texts; the book *Alcoholics Anonymous*, which is where the fellowship got its name, and *The Twelve Steps and Twelve Traditions,* written a few years later.

Wilson writes about being a chronic alcoholic who couldn't stay away from drinking. Then he had a spiritual experience that got him sober. Wilson wrote that the point of the book *Alcoholics Anonymous*, nicknamed the Big Book, is to give specific guidance about how to have a spiritual experience that can help other alcoholics stop drinking.

There's plenty about God in the Big Book. But not every one of the early members of AA believed in God. There was discussion, as there often is between alcoholics who can't agree. And the evolving understanding of how to communicate the path to a spiritual experience shifted away from a purely Christian, monotheistic portrayal of the Divine.

The Big Book says you don't have to believe in God to have a spiritual experience. You don't have to believe in any outside concept of the Divine. You can choose our own Higher Power. You can make up, refine and evolve your understanding of the Divine. Agnostics and atheists can have spiritual experiences that change their lives.

In this way, Wilson made AA's spiritual tools accessible to people who didn't believe in God, or didn't believe in a Christian Deity. Why not take that same approach to the spiritual tools of the Exercises to make them accessible to people who might have trouble with the religion, dogma or cultural perspective of the Saint?

I tried using the Drunk's lens of choosing your own conception of a Higher Power to refine the Saint's Exercises with friends and clients. Two young friends, both women in their early twenties, found this approach helpful. Neither has a structured spiritual practice, but both wanted to pass this content onto their friends. "We're coming out of a global pandemic, and we don't want to work the way we used to," one said. "We don't want to work the way our parents did, but we're not sure what to do next."

One of my clients, a high-powered CEO, worked through this content in a planning session with me and then asked if he could take the handouts home to his partner, who was making a big decision in her life. It seemed like the Saint's Exercises filtered through the lens of a choose-your-own-Higher Power could help people starting out in careers or well-established in leadership.

The goal of this book is to give you tools to make decisions in an intentional way, in a way that is congruent with your values. My hope is that these tools can work for you if you are an atheist or agnostic, spiritual but not religious, or a nun, rabbi, or imam. Anyone can benefit from a mindfulness practice adapted from the Buddhist tradition, and many people who participate in yoga as physical exercise may not need to understand more about the roots of yoga as a spiritual practice to find renewal.

While it's built on a spiritual framework, this is meant to be a practical book. Since many of us need to make decisions about what kind of work we are going to do, that will be a focus of this book. Which means I'll talk about money, and family, and who picks up the kids from day care. I'm not going to tell you to work harder or get a side hustle. I'm also not going to pretend that you can just manifest your way to a job that pays for your family's basic needs.

I will also give examples of ways this process can be used to make decisions about other aspects your life. I use a discernment process for every major decision in my life, and over time it's become a part of how I think, a kind of template for honoring my own internal promptings.

The Framework of this Book

The Foundation

The first part of this book summarizes the key elements of both Ignatius' and Wilson's writing that I will build upon for the rest of the book as well as useful concepts from their respective theologies. It will also give you a quick look at my social location as well as the principles I used in building this work.

The Beginning

First, understand specifically what question you want answered. What decision are you trying to make? If you don't know the answer to this yet, don't worry, as long as you have a general sense of what you are discerning.

Next, we'll look at practical considerations that can impact your decision. What are the financial responsibilities, health considerations, and family obligations that you want to consider? Are you sure those are all yours to own? We'll try to get to a personal map of facts for you to review.

Then we'll examine your values. What are the key things that motivate, sustain or connect you? For some this will be obvious, for others it may take some searching.

We will then consider what you know about yourself, your personality, style and preferences. When making a decision, looking at what you already know about yourself can be a fruitful area of focus when deciding what you might want to do next.

Stories that Support and Hinder

For many of us, our understanding of what we really want is obscured by stories we were told by our family or the dominant culture about what we should or should not want; what we can and cannot do. When we believe the limiting stories, it can restrain us. The stories that crop up most frequently are about work, money, quitting, power, home and family, voice, spirituality, rest, and the seasons of life. I'll review these so you can see if there are any old narratives you might need to reframe. We'll also look for helpful or supporting stories. While each of the short chapters may spark some ideas for you, you may also decide just to skip to the ones that you know are most relevant.

New Ways of Listening

Then we'll review different ways to listen to yourself and explore how to use your body and imagination for the deep listening discernment invites us to do. The intellect is a great tool, but limited, and we'll explore other potential channels.

Resistance and Support

Sometimes we run into emotional roadblocks on the way, and we'll review what they can be and how to accept them or work with them. Past traumas, especially those we carry in our bodies, as well as grief, can change how we move through a decision-making process.

Finally, we'll talk about ways to support yourself through the process, from building community to the Quaker practice of clearness committees.

How to use this book

This book is meant to be a starting point, a collection of suggestions. Since the process of discernment means we listen deeply to ourselves, I would invite you to listen to yourself as you engage with this material. Skip to whatever chapter or section calls to you or start at the beginning and go page by page. Dive deeply into one area and then skip another entirely. You can engage with this content in whatever way you feel called to encounter it. You know what it is that you need. Trust your knowing.

For those of you who like structure and direction, I would suggest that you sit with the questions under "Invitation to Explore" at the end of many of the chapters, which include some reflection and meditation exercises. You may want to write about what the questions evoke in you or your answers to each question, or what the meditations call forth.

I appreciate the idea of a spiritual curriculum intentionally practicing something each day, which I learned from the Jewish practice of Mussar, which I did with my friend Juliette a few years ago. In Mussar we focus on one virtue at a time, and may begin the day with a prayer or reading about the virtue, consider it throughout the day, and end the day writing about how we interacted with that virtue during the day. After a period of time, we move onto another virtue. That could be a useful way to sit with this content, as a kind of spiritual curriculum that you consider in different ways throughout your day or week.

This process is meant to take time. You can decide how long it will take for you, but it is better when not rushed. I understand it is countercultural to suggest we take our time and linger over content in a world of scrolling and newsfeeds. But sometimes slow spirituality is most nourishing.

A note on the texts

I used the translation of *Spiritual Exercises of St Ignatius* by Louis J Puhl, SJ, and the Third Edition of the book *Alcoholics Anonymous.* Both Ignatius and Wilson were men writing many years before an awareness of sexist language. I have elected not to alter their writing, which uses male pronouns and the word God or Higher Power to refer to the Divine and male pronouns to refer to universal experiences.

Where I quote the work directly, I refer to the *Spiritual Exercises of St Ignatius* as SE and reference the numbered stanzas that are traditionally used to reference sections of the *Spiritual Exercises of St Ignatius* across translations. When referencing text from *Alcoholics Anonymous* I will use BB and then the page number. The *Twelve Steps and Twelve Traditions* will be 12x12. Another foundational text is by Jim Harbaugh S.J. *A 12 Step Approach to the Spiritual Exercises of Ignatius* which I will refer to as Harbaugh.

Part One

The Foundation

CHAPTER ONE

What is discernment?

Discernment is a spiritual practice in which we listen for guidance. If mindfulness is turning your awareness to the present moment, then discernment is asking your question in every present moment and looking around for the answers, confident that they will arrive, even if they are cloaked or veiled. Like mindfulness, discernment is a practice that is hard to describe fully and difficult to do consistently, but when you get it, you know it. Regular practice is how you get it. The point of this book is to help you develop a discernment practice that you can use for the rest of your life.

I think of discernment as a kind of spiritual scavenger hunt. You're searching for an answer. You have a set of instructions, but they are vague and can be interpreted multiple ways, like clues or riddles. And it's a long scavenger hunt. As you go along, you develop the habit of looking for clues. You look for clues in unlikely places, and when you find them, it reinforces the habit of looking. You show up in the world with curiosity about the world and yourself, holding in mind what you want to learn, and you wait for guidance.

Discernment is often used to describe the process by which an individual decides if a religious vocation or a call to vowed religious life is for them. But it can be useful for those of us who aren't called to be spiritual leaders in any faith tradition. Because how we work in the world can be a vocation and ministry, no matter what we do. It matters to us. It matters to our family. It matters to the people around us. Why shouldn't we honor our work with the same intentionality that others honor a religious vocation?

What do I want to do in the world? What am I called to do? How can I help the people around me?

Often when we are making a decision about what kind of career to pursue, what educational field or degree to work towards or how we want to spend the period of time after we retire, we are steered towards intellectual approaches, like a list of pros and cons. There are plenty of assessments that can measure your skills sets and aptitudes, and they can be helpful.

But some of us want a deeper process, something that taps into our spiritual, ethical and intentional framework. We value the intellectual, but we also believe there is wisdom in the body, in community, in art and philosophy or our faith tradition. We may have deeply held convictions about how we want to spend our time and resources, or specific values we want to live out or communities we want to help, or ways we want to care for the earth.

We don't want to just decide, we want to discern. We want to bring our values, our beliefs, our lived experience, our body and spirit into the process, not just the intellect. The process of discernment does just that.

And for people who believe in God, or any manifestation of the Divine, including Ancestors or Nature, discernment is a way to get direction about how you can be of service to the world, guidance from the Universe about how you are invited to help the Universe.

Like other spiritual practices, discernment isn't a paint-by-numbers exercise. It has a life of its own. It is a process, yes, one that has been used by many people over centuries. But engaging with the Numinous is unpredictable. It's more like gardening than building an engine. Some plants flourish, others wither. A late frost, a heat wave, or a crop of pests can undermine the most assiduous gardening plan. I have brought specific problems to discernment and found the question I was asking wasn't what I needed to know at all, and the whole landscape changed in unexpected ways. It can be frustrating and delightful to be reminded that we aren't in charge in the way we might have thought.

CHAPTER TWO

The Saint

Who was Ignatius of Loyola?

Ignatius was born in 1491 and became a mercenary. He was not, in his early life, a particularly holy guy. In the first lines of his autobiography, he described himself in this way: "Up to his twenty-sixth year the heart of Ignatius was enthralled by the vanities of the world. His special delight was in the military life, and he seemed led by a strong and empty desire of gaining for himself a great name."[1] In May of 1521 he was struck by a cannonball which broke one leg and wounded the other. Since he wanted to continue to be a soldier to engage in "his special delight" he opted for additional surgeries and a longer time recuperating so he could regain full function in both legs. He recuperated at his family's home, which was a small castle in northern Spain, and had few books to read, all religious texts.

He started to consider a life devoted to God. He was trying to decide what to do once he was healed. Priest or soldier? Holy man or mercenary? He noticed that when he thought about devoting his life to God, he felt good. When he daydreamed about returning to the battlefield, or "what he should do in honor of an illustrious lady, how he should journey to the city where she was, in what words he would address her, and what bright and pleasant sayings he would make use of, what manner of warlike exploits he should perform to please her." [2] he felt good about that as well. Thinking about serving God made him feel good in a specific way. It was sustaining and sustained. It lasted in a steady flow. "When he thought of worldly things it gave him great pleasure, but afterward he found himself dry and sad."[3]

This was to become the foundation for the Spiritual Exercises. Ignatius thought of the Exercises as similar to physical exercise. "For just as taking a walk,

[1] The Project Gutenberg eBook of The Autobiography of St. Ignatius, by Saint Ignatius Loyola
[2] Ibid Chapter One
[3] Ibid Chapter One

journeying on foot, and running are bodily exercises, so we call Spiritual Exercises every way of preparing and disposing the soul to rid itself of all inordinate attachments, and after their removal, seeking and finding the will of God in the disposition of our life . . ." (SE #1) He gave very specific directions for how to do these exercises, the way a trainer might outline a set of physical exercises to increase flexibility. The result is a process for listening and observing the internal movements of one's imagination, mind and spirit developed by a soldier with a broken leg who was stuck in a drafty castle.

The concept of "inordinate attachments" is central to Ignatian thought. The Buddhist tradition also attends to the spiritual challenges of attachment. Clinging to people, situations, narratives or material goods causes suffering. Ignatius also explored the need to get rid of all our inordinate attachments in order to be able to clearly see what we are to do.

Ignatius decided to devote himself to God, and leave behind his life as a mercenary. But Ignatius went about it with a misguided fervor for a solitary spiritual life. For almost a year, he spent much of his time in prayer in a cave, living as a beggar and eating little.

"Ignatius, after coming close to suicide because of his ferocious spiritual regimen, consulted a spiritual director, who brought him back down to earth and helped him to rejoin the human race." (Harbaugh p. xiv) Ignatius decided to return to school and study, which he did for another twelve years, an older soldier studying with young men. But the young men were intrigued with his Spiritual Exercises, the instructions he had written to help others replicate the process he himself had undergone. He founded the Jesuits, or the Order of the Society of Jesus. They exist today, in fact, the current Catholic Pope, Francis, is a Jesuit.

The Spiritual Exercises are predicated on the idea that any one of us can go directly to the Divine and get guidance. Yes, the Jesuit order is part of the Catholic Church. Ignatius was very much a Catholic. But what's radical and useful to me in the context of this book is the idea that there is a direct channel between each of us and the Divine that will allow us to get guidance. We don't need an interlocutor or go-between, a priest or any other spiritual leader. In his "Introductory Observations" Ignatius speaks directly to the person who is taking someone through the Exercises and says that the director shouldn't get in the way of God's direct communication with the person going through the Exercises "to permit the Creator to deal directly with the creature and the creature directly with his Creator and Lord." (SE #15). Stop and consider that this was written by a Catholic priest in the 16th century, telling a spiritual director, who would have often been a priest, not to get in the way of God directly communicating with the person doing the Exercises.

The Spiritual Exercises are divided into four sections, called "weeks," and focus on meditations on biblical stories of episodes in the life of Jesus, inviting us to consider aspects of how those stories guide us to a new or changed understanding of our call or vocation in the world.

In this book, I am not following the format of the weeks, nor will I be referring to the biblical texts. There are many excellent resources for people who are interested in using the Spiritual Exercises as a religious retreat. I am taking some of the fundamentals of the Spiritual Exercises and Ignatian Spirituality and using them as a foundation upon which anyone can build a practice of discernment.

Discernment is a way of making decisions that is intentional and spiritual. Ignatius then, and the Jesuits now, believe that the Spiritual Exercises can help you understand what God wants you to do in the world. I find the process of discernment useful for anyone looking for a values based, intentional process for making decisions. Here are a few other Jesuit concepts that are foundational to the Exercises, Jesuit spirituality and this book.

Imaginative Contemplation

One of the key techniques that Ignatius uses is embodied imaginative contemplation. He calls it Application of the Senses. He suggests that we imagine that we are in a biblical scene. In quiet contemplation, we are to imagine every aspect of what being in our body in such a scene would be like. Is it dusty? Is it hot? Am I thirsty? What does the chair feel like where Jesus just sat? Who would I be in the scene? I then sit quietly and imagine what my body is experiencing through my senses. Then I get curious about what is coming up for me emotionally. Do I feel angry? Sad? I'm just observing, uncritically, and if there is nothing arising for me, I just sit quietly in that imagined space.

In that long ago conversation I had with Danielle in the white conference room with the grand piano, this was the technique I explained to her. She was trying to discern if she should leave her career in advertising and become a photographer. I suggested that she quiet her mind and imagine her day as a photographer. What would it feel like to wake up if that was her job? How did she feel about going to work in the morning? What was it like to go through the day? I invited her to go into as much detail as she wanted, to really paint a picture for herself, to envision the scenes in detail. Then see how she felt in her body. Check in with her emotional ecosystem as she went through this exercise. Go all the way through to the end of the day, returning home in her imagination and looking back on her imagined day. How did she feel? I suggested she then do the same exercise for continuing to stay in her existing job.

I have been surprised at what comes up for me when I am in this state of embodied imaginative contemplation. Sometimes the feedback I get from myself is garbled, like listening to a foreign language I'm studying when it's spoken by a native speaker. At first, I can only catch a word here and there. Then I get better and can sometimes understand sentences. Now imagine that the native speaker you are trying to communicate with is someone you love who loves you but who can't speak your language. Imagine how intently you would be listening, how you would take in not just the words which you don't know yet, but the intonation, the body movements, the hand gestures. You'd learn pretty quickly in that attitude. It can be the same with learning discernment.

The Divine is in all things, including us

Everything is sacred, including you and me. Our work, our family life, our bodies, our minds. Holy, holy, holy. The term "vocation" is usually used to talk about vowed religious, nuns, priests, pastors. I've widened the aperture for vocation to include our work in the world. And I use work expansively – parenting is work, grandparenting is work, caregiving is work, relationships with others are work, being part of community is work, art is work. If we believe that our work is sacred, that we are ministering to one another in all our interactions, would we take decisions we make about work or how we connect to others more seriously? Would we be more intentional?

It's a change of heart

The intellectual is always useful, but in Ignatian spirituality intellect is not more important than heart and spirit. Our society tends to privilege the intellect. Great passions of the heart, the sense that we must do a thing or follow a certain path, are important, even if they can't be justified or validated by intellect or the culture in which we live. Ignatius had big feelings, and he tried things that sometimes failed[4].

[4] https://www.ignatianspirituality.com/ignatian-prayer/the-spiritual-exercises/a-spirituality-of-the-heart/

Ignatius wasn't teaching theology. He was sharing how he reoriented himself. He changed his heart and in doing that changed his orientation to the world. And that's what he was trying to teach others in the Exercises; how we can respond more faithfully to what we are called to do and to be.

If you, like me, grew up in a culture that privileged the intellect, words, reason, and rationality, it may feel odd to put that frame of reference aside and try to listen with different ears, see with different eyes. It helps me to think about it as a two-way process, a co-creation. I'm not doing this alone. There is another energy available, inviting and helping me. Again, we can call that energy God, our Ancestors, our Higher Self, Nature. As we move deeply into the question, we will find that we are given insights that can feel like they come from outside us, or from such a deep place within us that they still surprise.

Community and direction

We are meant to be in community, and this is especially true when we are trying to understand how to be in the world. But it's often difficult to find community, especially if you're not part of a specific religious tradition. Then again, I've been part of churches that never felt like community to me, even though I went every Sunday. And I've seen a group of women knitting around a table in a yarn store that felt like a wonderful community. You can also make your own community. In-person interactions are great, but communities of people online can also be supportive. You can build your own intentional communities.

As you go through discernment, it is best to have individual direction, so you have a person to talk to about your specific desires and dreams and discoveries. Career coaches, spiritual directors, and counselors can all be useful guides. But those may not be available to everyone for various reasons. Or you may not feel that one of those is right for you at this time.

If you're called to do this work on your own, without community or one on one direction, that's fine. But please keep yourself open to building community, however small, and finding a trusted advisor to talk to about what comes up for you. It doesn't have to be a trained professional. I often talk with my Aunt Tanya about spiritual matters and career or financial decisions. She's known me since I was born, we share similar values, we talk often, and I trust her. If you're lucky enough to have an Aunt Tanya in your life, give her a call, let her know what you're doing.

The discernment of spirits

The discernment of spirits is a process of understanding our interior experiences. It's a way of noticing and paying attention to what is happening in our inner life. Ignatius believed that he had good spirits and evil spirits inside of him, all telling him which way to go. He wanted to understand how to tell the good voices from the bad ones.

To me, discernment of spirits is about understanding where we are prioritizing greed, fear, selfishness or resentment over values like compassion, generosity, empathy or trust. At other times, it's about understanding and examining old scripts we carry. Most of us have an experience of negative "voices" in our head, interior messages that lead us in the wrong direction, or justify unskillful behavior. I call them my Inner Community, and I'll talk more about that in Chapter Eleven. We also may have positive messages that replay about our divine nature, our worth, or our innate value as a person.

Rather than evil spirits, I find that often what obscures my understanding are narratives, cultural assumptions and worldviews. I'm trying to find the map that will take me to the buried treasure of understanding what my work in the world is going to be. I don't have to fix anything, or judge anything, I just need to find the map to get to the treasure, where I will find abundance and direction. Negative narratives can be stains on that map that obscure where I'm going, and I need to address them to see my way more clearly.

To do that I have to understand what supports that journey and what works against it. The discernment of spirits will, in our context, mean getting better at understanding what supports us and what does not.

The Exercises as a feminist practice

To me, the Exercises are a deeply feminist practice, although that might not be readily apparent when reading the text of *The Spiritual Exercises* because Ignatius carries the sexism of his era.

But his teachings are very feminist. First, it assumes I can develop a direct relationship with the Divine and get specific guidance from that relationship. I don't need any mediator. No priest, guru, teacher or learning is required. I have a connection already. It exists, it is the ground of my being. It might be obscured or clouded, but that surface can be cleaned, like a window that, wiped of dirt, lets in the sun again.

Second, while my intellect is involved, ways of knowing that involve the body, senses, Spirit, imagination and feelings are privileged. My body matters. It has wisdom. The practice centers the wisdom of the body. There is no duality, no body or intellect, mind or heart.

Rest where you find fruit

"Rest where you find fruit" is a common Jesuit refrain. It means that when you find a spiritual practice or type of prayer or worship that is fruitful for you, keep doing it. When it stops feeling fruitful, move onto something else. You are the one who decides. You are the authority on what it is that serves you. I find this so freeing. Not only can I trust my body, I can trust my understanding. If something works, keep doing it. If something doesn't work anymore move on. What works for another might not work for me, and what works for me might not work for another.

I invite you take that attitude as you read this book. If something resonates or is useful, dwell there. If there's no fruit for you, if a concept or approach doesn't engage you, then let it go and move onto another section.

Consolation and desolation

The Exercises take time. Jesuit spirituality understands that there are seasons in any spiritual practice. Another Jesuit concept I appreciate is the idea of consolation and desolation. In short, this recognizes that our spiritual life has seasons which are largely outside of our control. We shouldn't worry about the changing emotional weather or try to force a change.

Consolation is when you feel spiritually connected and spiritual practice makes you feel good. Until it doesn't. In desolation, you don't feel close to Spirit or Source. Spiritual practice may be dry or unsatisfying. You haven't done anything wrong, there's no sin or turning away, it's just that the connection feels interrupted, unstable.

The gift of the Jesuit idea of desolation is that feeling stuck and disconnected in any spiritual process, whether it's going through this book or being married, is an integral part of the spiritual process. It's not a failing on our part any more than it is a failing of nature that winter where I live is cold and rainy. It is the season. An ongoing period of desolation is called a Dark Night of the Soul, from

St. John of the Cross. That also isn't "our fault" but a sign of our continued spiritual growth and maturity.

These are deep spiritual concepts that I can't do justice to in a few short paragraphs. The point is that there are going to be ups and downs, and it's part of the process, so we shouldn't worry too much about it.

CHAPTER THREE

The Drunk

Bill Wilson, the co-founder of Alcoholics Anonymous, was born in 1895. He, like Ignatius, was a soldier and fought in World War I. He was also an alcoholic. He tried many ways to stay sober, but wasn't able to maintain continuous sobriety. Then one day, lying in bed in a hospital, he had a spiritual experience. He said he heard the voice of God say to him "Who are you to say there is no God," and he was so overwhelmed he fell to the floor. (BB p. 56). He never took another drink of alcohol.

In 1934 he met a doctor named Bob Smith who was also an alcoholic. Together they started what would become Alcoholics Anonymous. Wilson was the author of the book *Alcoholics Anonymous*, from which the group got its name, and a few years later of the book *The Twelve Steps and Twelve Traditions*, which elaborated on the information about the Twelve Steps outlined in the book *Alcoholics Anonymous*, as well as the Twelve Traditions, which are guides to the functioning of AA. Others influenced the content of the book, and there is no listed author, but it is generally accepted that Wilson was the primary author.

The Twelve Steps are a spiritual practice with twelve activities or steps, done in order, with a sponsor or guide. The result of the steps is a spiritual experience sufficient to enable a person to stop using the alcohol, drugs or whatever substance or behavior they are addicted to, their "inordinate attachments." The Twelve Steps are also the basis of AlAnon Family Groups for the friends and family members of alcoholics and addicts. While those close to the alcoholic or addict might not engage in any addictive behaviors around substances, they consider themselves to have been impacted by the family disease of alcoholism or addiction and have found that working the same Twelve Steps allows them to detach from their addicted loved one and maintain balance and stability even when someone they love is still in the throes of their disease.

The Twelve Steps are done in community. Support groups or meetings as well as interactions with others in recovery, are considered by researchers to be a key reason that AA is as effective as it is in helping people stay clean and sober. [1] The fellowship is effective, the spiritual program is effective, but both together work well for many people.

AA is not the only way to get clean and sober. Many find that complete abstinence from alcohol is too demanding, and others are put off by the spirituality, which is often spoken of in specifically Christian, American language. When AA began in 1935 it was one of the few ways alcoholics could get sober, but in the intervening decades many treatment options, including prescription drugs which aid greatly in harm reduction by limiting the effect of drugs and alcohol, have revolutionized the options for people with a substance abuse disorder.

What I find surprising is that AA works at all. That even one late-stage alcoholic living under a bridge can have a change of heart so significant that he can get and stay sober and return to his family and society; that one heroin addict can find a community and a spiritual solution robust enough to enable her to stay clean for decades is amazing. We have become so used to portrayals of AA in TV shows and dramas, as part of the cultural landscape, that I think we lose sight of what it can do. If you've ever known an alcoholic or addict deep in the throes of their disease, ready to risk family, love, children, job, freedom, self-respect, even life itself in pursuit of that addiction, think about that person. Wouldn't it be amazing if they could stop doing that, if they found a way to never do that thing again, and return, changed, to the world?

The Drunk and the Saint

A Jesuit priest named Ed Dowling read the text *Alcoholics Anonymous* soon after it was written and reached out to Wilson. Wilson writes that Dowling showed up late one stormy night and rousted Wilson out of bed. Wilson and his wife Lois were living above an AA gathering space, and she was out for the evening. Wilson thought Dowling was another drunk seeking help until he saw that Dowling was sober and wearing a clerical collar. Dowling told Wilson he thought the Twelve Steps of AA looked like the Spiritual Exercises of Ignatius of Loyola. He became a friend and spiritual advisor to Wilson, and an early proponent of AA. Wilson wasn't Catholic. Dowling wasn't an alcoholic. It didn't matter to their friendship.[2]

1 https://med.stanford.edu/news/all-news/2020/03/alcoholics-anonymous-most-effective-path-to-alcohol-abstinence.html

2 https://www.aa.org/sites/default/files/newsletters/en_box459_aug-sept06.pdf

Lots of people have gotten sober without ever knowing the connection Father Dowling saw between the Twelve Steps and the Exercises. I didn't know it when I got sober. Then I met a Jesuit priest named Jim Harbaugh, SJ. He wrote a book called *A 12-Step Approach to the Spiritual Exercises of St Ignatius*. I read it. It connected the dots for me, between my father's reverence for Jesuit thought, intellect and inquiry, my sobriety, and my curiosity about spiritual tools and practices.

I did the Spiritual Exercises, over a period of months, with a Spiritual Director. We met once a month and I committed to an hour a day of prayer and Bible readings. My Bible still has the readings for each month's study written on the fly leaf. An hour of prayer a day seems like a lot, especially because I was a single parent with two kids in middle school, but I did it. I don't remember any big spiritual experiences or revelations. My ultimate discernment was that I should keep on doing what I was doing – raising my children and working to support them and the stable life I was building for them.

What I didn't know at the time was that I was developing a set of skills that would become part of my neural network, in my muscle memory. I was learning how to listen to the movements of my heart, my spirit, my body. I was learning how to discern.

As Harbaugh points out in the introduction to his book *A 12 Step Approach to the Spiritual Exercises of St Ignatius,* there are many similarities between Bill Wilson's writing and that of Saint Ignatius. They both believe people can profoundly change their lives and understanding through a spiritual experience. "Central both to 'the 12 Step approach' and to the Spiritual Exercises is the notion that what is most needed if a human being wants to move from misery to contentment is a thorough conversion." (Harbaugh p. xv)

"Both Bill and Ignatius believe that conversion can be evoked, or facilitated, by a methodical, highly structured approach; indeed, both approaches have been criticized for being too regimented. Both the *Spiritual Exercises* and *Alcoholics Anonymous* assume that conversion begins with a deep sense of human brokenness." (Harbaugh p. xv) Both men set out clear, specific instructions for a process to get to that spiritual experience which is strong enough to change our minds, our hearts and our lives.

One of the key differences is that Ignatius grounds his process in the life of Jesus Christ and assumes participation in the Catholic Church. Wilson and the early members of AA believed differently. "Prospective members were told that they could regard their spiritual experiences in any way that made sense to them – it was to be God as they understood God. Atheist and agnostic members were welcome." (Harbaugh p. xvi)

In the Big Book, there are multiple references to using spiritual tools to make a decision. The most well-known is: "In meditation, we asked God what we should do about each specific matter. The right answer will come, if we want it." (BB p.69)

Here are some of the concepts from Twelve Step spirituality that I find useful, and which underpin the ideas in this book.

A Higher Power

In AA everyone is encouraged to find a Power greater than themselves. It should be their own conception, and it can be anything. Recovering alcoholics like acronyms and for those leery of "the God thing" there is G.O.D. as Good Orderly Direction or Group of Drunks. "Do not let any prejudice you may have against spiritual terms deter you from honestly asking yourself what they mean to you." (BB p. 47)

You can establish a direct connection with this Higher Power. And that connection can guide and sustain you. Even if you are an atheist. Which can be a bit hard to get your head around. What you believe is not as important as what you do. Taking action, helping others, and going through the process of the Twelve Steps will lead to a spiritual awakening which can change the direction of your life. Step Twelve reads "Having had a spiritual awakening as the result of these steps . . ." (BB p. 60)

That's the similarity with the Ignatian Exercises. Follow this recipe and you'll get a result. Do these things, described in detail but with lots of room for individual interpretation and this other thing will occur, a profound change of heart, which can change your life.

It will be uncomfortable

Throughout the Big Book there are references to the discomfort and resistance a spiritual process can produce. "All of us, without exception, pass through times when we can pray only with the greatest exertion of will. Occasionally we go even further than this. We are faced with a rebellion so sickening that we simply won't pray. When these things happen, we should not think too ill of ourselves. We should simply resume prayer as soon as we can." (12X12 p.105)

In reference to taking the Twelve Steps, Wilson writes "Many of us exclaimed, 'What an order! I can't go through with it.' Do not be discouraged, No one among us has been able to maintain anything like perfect adherence to these principles. We are not saints. The point is, that we are willing to grow along spiritual lines." (BB p 60)

The multiple references to alcoholics balking at self-examination, making amends, or continuing to grow spiritually treat resistance as a given on any spiritual path. We're going to balk. Don't make too big of a deal about it and try to get back on track when you can.

Identification at Depth

Identification at depth is the belief that one alcoholic can understand another alcoholic, in spite of vast differences that would otherwise keep them apart. They can identify "at depth." I can talk to another alcoholic, and we can understand each other quickly. The other alcoholic may be very different from me in every way, but if we share the disease of alcoholism, we can connect at depth.

I've noticed this in other arenas as well. A person who has a lived experience of a particular set of circumstances can connect more deeply with another person who has also experienced that same set of circumstances. It might be mental illness, bereavement, prejudice, discrimination, incarceration, health challenges, but that moment when you connect with someone who has gone through similar experiences can be deep and sustaining. Identification at depth can be a strong connection upon which to build community.

Working with others

A key part of recovery in Twelve Step programs is working with other people who struggle with the same addictions or challenges. Carrying the message, as it's also called, means taking other people through the process of the Twelve Steps and generally supporting people within your community of recovery.

This presupposes a community. Whether it's an AA hall in a gritty industrial area or an AlAnon Family Group meeting on Zoom, or a Narcotics Anonymous meeting in a church basement, Twelve Step programs happen in community. Some people believe that it is the community as much as the spiritual program that heals. Our world is having an epidemic of loneliness, and that's contributing to addiction and the deaths of despair. You can see why connection with a group of people trying to move away from despair together could be helpful.

But the spiritual and emotional benefits of working with others can be sustained even without community. Helping another person in any small way can improve our spiritual life and connection, and make us feel better, assuming, of course, that we are operating with strong personal boundaries.

Humility

AA has humility as an organization. AA doesn't say AA is the only way to stay sober. To the contrary, it says that this is only one approach. The organization "has no opinion on outside issues" and avoids "public controversy". "Our leaders are but trusted servants, they do not govern." (BB p. 564)

In other words, no matter how long a person has been sober, no matter what sort of status they think they have, they don't have all the answers. There are no gurus, no experts, no authority. In fact, AA is not governed in any traditional way that most would recognize. "For our group purpose there is but one ultimate authority – a loving God as He may express Himself in our group conscience." (BB p.564). A group conscience is a vote, taking place in "business meetings." There is extensive conversation, a priority given to hearing from those who disagree with the majority, and then everyone gets an equal vote. Because, fundamentally, we don't need an authority. Both Wilson and Ignatius wrote incredibly detailed instructions for each of us to find and connect with a Higher Power to guide us through our lives. And Wilson and the early AAs believed that same Power could guide the organization.

Humility informs the principle of anonymity. It is suggested that people who are members of AA don't talk about that membership in public, that they "maintain personal anonymity at the level of press, radio and films." (BB p. 564). The arch references to "friends in church basements" or "recovery" may seem like splitting hairs, but any spiritual principle that suggests people keep quiet about their accomplishments feels refreshing in this age of social media, and a movement away from ego. Anonymity is not about shame, it's about humility, an acknowledgment that even the most famous recovering alcoholic or addict, even someone with decades of sobriety, is still an addict or alcoholic and can start drinking or using again anytime.

The guide

Ignatius and the Jesuits as well as Bill Wilson and the recovering alcoholics and addicts he influenced all advise a guide for this process. In AA that's called a sponsor. For Ignatius and the Jesuits that's a spiritual director, or the leader of a retreat. These are people who understand the spiritual process you are undertaking, and can help you along the way. Sometimes they can keep us from making bad decisions. "Being still inexperienced and having just made conscious contact with God, it is not probable that we are going to be inspired at all times. We might pay for this presumption in all sorts of absurd actions and ideas." (BB p 87).

A guide can also help you manage emotions or energy that may arise. In a class I took in graduate school, Ronald Rolheiser, OMI, a priest and theologian, said that sexuality and spirituality are such strong forces that humans have tried to manage them by hemming them in with structure and ritual. The container for sexuality was marriage, the container for spirituality was religion. Spirituality unchecked, he said, could be used for harm, as when the followers of Jim Jones took their lives en masse with poison mixed in KoolAid because Jones told them to do it. It's not hard to think of ways in which spirituality, the longing for greater meaning, connection, purpose and community has been misused by people in power trying to pervert that strong force and desire to their own ends. I don't think that either sexuality or spirituality needs to be strictly regulated in cultural or religious containers. But I also think we need to be respectful of their intensity, just as sailors respect the sea.

In addition to the Spiritual Exercises, I have a long practice with Centering Prayer. I've had spiritual directors for many years, and they have had to explain some of my experiences to me. The strong force that is spirituality can create disturbances so acute that they feel like mental illness. Thomas Keating, a Trappist monk who wrote extensively about Centering Prayer described these feelings as "psychic nausea." I joked with my spiritual director at the time I experienced "psychic nausea" that it was more like psychic puking, and that she was the one holding my hair back as I threw up. She was a nun and a recovering alcoholic, so she found that funny.

So, yes, ideally you would have a guide through this process, or a trusted person to share your experiences with, especially if you discern something that entails a dramatic change to your life. If you decide that your Higher Power is telling you to sell everything you own and move to a faraway country, you might be right, but it's a good idea to run that by someone who has more experience than you do with the Divine, discernment and life changes. Recovering alcoholics often tell a newly sober person that if they have a great idea, they should tell their sponsor that great idea before they do it. It's the same principle here.

A guide can also correct any natural inclinations you may have to misinterpret reality or misread yourself. We'll talk later in Chapter Eleven about the Inner

Community, the set of messages and attitudes we carry in our heads. Mine mostly say I'm an idiot and what do I think I'm doing speaking up. Some people have an Inner Community that says they are victims and shouldn't have to show up and do adult life. Others may give mixed messages. That's where a guide, elder or friend can help reconnect you to a more balanced view of your responsibilities and abilities.

If I'm the only guide you have for this process, meaning me as the author of this book, rather than me if you know me, then I'll try to be mindful of pointing out places that might be difficult, or thought traps I've fallen into or where I've seen others stumble. And overall, I'll try to follow the explicit instructions Ignatius provides in his introduction for the person leading this process, liberally adapted by me:

- Be brief. Hit the high points and let the thoughts of the person doing the work (that's you), possibly influenced by the Divine, lead them to a deeper understanding.
- Get out of the way and let a Higher Power as the person understands their Higher Power connect with them directly.
- Make sure that these exercises can be accessible to many; "adapted to the condition of the one who is to engage in them, that is, to his age, education and talent." (SE #18). In other words, I'll put some ideas in front of you, and you can choose which are best suited to the particular "condition" in which you find yourself.

CHAPTER FOUR

Social Location

When I was in graduate school (at Seattle University, a Jesuit University, in the now defunct School of Theology and Ministry) I was told that everything I wrote should include my social location so that the reader could place me and understand what privilege and experience color my understanding. I like that idea. If you're going to come along with me, you should know what influences my perceptions.

I'm a white woman, born in 1962, a second-generation Italian American. As I was growing up, my family moved often for my father's job at IBM, until he became sick when I was in high school. He died of a rare heart disease in his forties, when I was nineteen. When he died, I was adrift. I married at twenty-one because it offered a kind of instant identity and purpose. I had two kids right away, a boy named RJ and a girl named Emma. I divorced and became a single parent when they were quite young.

I'm a recovering alcoholic, and I've been sober for a long time.

I was Catholic for most of my life. I became an Episcopalian in my fifties. I'm an Associate of the Sisters of St Joseph of Peace, an order of Catholic nuns committed to peace through justice. An Associate is a lay person who is connected to the work, or charism, of an order, but doesn't take formal vows. In other orders they are called Oblates, or Third Order, or Tertiaries. I think of myself as nun-adjacent.

I am a bereaved parent. My son RJ was in a car accident in 2003 and sustained a traumatic brain injury. He died in 2005.

I worked in advertising and technology for decades, in sales and business development and, later, in management. It wasn't a great experience for me. I've become disillusioned with capitalism, especially how it manifests in those industries. After completing an MA in Transformational Leadership, I started my consultancy and career as an executive coach ten years ago.

Group Agreements

When I begin work with a group of people, whether it's an ongoing engagement or just a strategy session I'm facilitating, I like to start with Group Agreements. How do we want to work together? What are the principles we are following? Even though we can't do that as an actual group, since you all are separate and reading this at different times, I wanted to outline a few fundamental principles which guided me in developing this content and name them for our mutual orientation.

1. Each of us knows what is good for us, and what we are called to do. That understanding is in us, but it is often obscured by what we are told about who we are allowed to be. Sometimes trauma or old wounds get in the way. We aren't searching for or building something new or foreign or outside of us. We are revisiting, reconnecting or recapturing something we already have but may have lost track of along the way.
2. Our body has a genius. We can listen to our bodies and get additional ways of knowing and understanding. Have you ever met a person and quickly felt close to them? Just had a sense of calm and peace when you were near them? Have you ever fallen in love with someone and realized they smell wonderful to you? Have you ever held a newborn and had the baby snuggle up into you and felt that wave of connection, affection, love? This is our body knowing. Many of us are told not to trust or listen to anything that arises from our bodies, or we're told that our bodies are bad or wrong. It can be a challenge to get back to this source of wisdom, but it's good to understand that's where we are headed.
3. There is a force that is available to help us. Call it what you will; our Ancestors, the Divine under any name, Nature, our Higher Selves, our intuition. If you don't believe this, that's ok. This process will still work for you. I don't understand how gravity works, but it still keeps me connected to the ground.
4. We should honor our resistance. Even when we feel invited to greater understanding, we might need to pause along the path. There's an old saying "When the student is ready the teacher will appear." I like to add to that when the student is tired or sore on the journey, she should rest and refresh herself and honor her resistance. If I believe I know what's good for me in a deep fundamental way, I don't have to rush anything. I try not to

judge myself for needing to absorb new information slowly. I try to honor my resistance.

5. Our life is full of seasons. There are times where we are curious and connect with the world and others, and there are times when we retreat and relish solitude. There are times when our lives are full of family and the demands of caring for loved ones, and times where we can more fully consider our own needs and desires. There are times of grief, loss, illness, and pain. And there are times of joy, love, creativity, and celebration. This too shall pass, whatever it is, and it's not our "fault" either way. It's not about hustling more or harder, or being more positive or healing on a specific timeline. Nothing I can do can make summer longer or shorter. It can be the same with the seasons of life.
6. You are the expert on yourself. I'm just another person trying to figure things out. I'm sharing my experience, strength and hope with you to see if it might spark something in you. Everything I offer is an invitation, not a command; a suggestion, not an order. I have no authority. Neither does anyone else. You are the expert on you, your understanding of the Divine and your invitation to be in the world. Trust that.

Part Two

The Beginning

CHAPTER FIVE

What question do you want to ask?

What do you want to know?

When I begin this process with someone, they often think they are clear about what they want to know. But when we get into the specifics, they realize that their question is too vague to support the kind of investigation we are going to begin. In other cases, they start with one question and then discover another question as they go through the process. Let's start with your question. What question are you asking? If you know your question, you might want to think about it or write it down before reading further.

This discernment process is best for longer term decisions that will impact the direction of your life in a significant way. The discernment process can take months. What question do you want to sit with for weeks or even months? If you feel like the old "I'm standing at a fork in the road" cliche applies to you and your question, you're probably in the right arena.

Once, I did this discernment process to decide if I wanted to work for myself and what that work should be. I had a feeling that was what I wanted to do, but I was afraid of the financial insecurity that might follow. It's not unusual to feel conflicted, or as if different parts of you want different things. If we weren't conflicted in some way, then the decision would be easier, and we might not need to use the tools of discernment. In my case, my question was twofold: Do I want to work for myself? What kind of work do I want to do?

Spend time here. Don't rush. Here are a few sample questions to review.

"Do I want to leave medicine and find another career? What should that career be?"

"Do I want to go to graduate school?"

"Do I want to end my marriage?"

"Do I want to be a parent?"

I am intentionally framing these with the statement "I want." "What do I want?" is an important question when I believe what I want can be an expression of my deepest, truest, longing. Too often "I want" is dismissed as childish, selfish, immature. Try to approach your question without judgement. The question can evolve over time, and no one need see it besides you.

If you find during this process that another question arises, you can also capture that. The two questions may turn out to be related, and link later in this work. Or you may decide to put one question aside and focus on the other. Don't be concerned if more than one thing arises right now.

Work and Econ

A young friend who is an artist makes a distinction I quite like between what she does to make money to pay her bills and her work as an artist, which is her true focus. "Econ" is what she does to make money. "Work" is her art. Her work is the central point of focus, it's what's important to her. Econ is useful, and she is glad she has a trade that is portable and can provide for her financial needs. She finds her job cutting hair to be pleasant enough, but dancing is where she focuses most of her energy.

There are people lucky enough that the work they are called to do, where they feel alive, can also pay their bills. But many of us are not. My art is writing. Aside from my time as a journalist, the amount of money I have made writing my own words wouldn't buy a used car. I've ghost written plenty of content for other people and I understand that helped hone my skills. But my true work has never been my econ. Because of that, when I am deciding what kind of econ I want to do, I know that I need to make sure I have time to do my art, my true work.

When I was deciding if I wanted to work for myself, part of the reason I wanted to be self-employed was to have more time to write. While I was deciding an econ question – how do I support myself – it was in service to a true work goal – getting more time and space to write.

Most of what our society thinks of as work is econ. I invite you to expand your definition of work to include art of all kinds, as well as community service, studying, political activism, spiritual practice, sports, childcare or elder care, farming, education or learning, teaching, making, cooking, any craft. If you do something on this list that is meaningful to you and brings you joy, then it may be your true work, or your true work in this season of your life, in the case of caring for children or elders. Honor your true work, even if society or the people around you do not.

What if I don't know what I want to know?

I've also taken people through this process who don't know the specific contours of the question they are asking yet. They feel conflicted, they are restless and uncertain. Often, they have a sense of questioning what they've been doing, or who they have been told to be, or something important. But they can't quite put it into words, which can be frustrating. They are called to a discernment process, but can't quite get a grasp on what they are asking.

You can use the tools of discernment to refine the question you want to discern. So, if you don't know what you want to know yet, that's fine. Be with that. Your restlessness and dissatisfaction may be an invitation to explore other options or reframe key narratives. You can continue with this process and return to the question.

Space

I like to use ritual, symbolism and space to support this process. The spaces in which I engage in meditation, journaling or other exploration are all very intentionally constructed. The last time I went through this discernment process, I used a wall in my guest room. I took everything off the wall, so it was a blank slate. I purchased a bunch of sticky notes in different sizes and colors. I enjoy office supplies, they always remind me of the start of school, of fresh clean notebooks and new beginnings. I bought a box of colored pens. I put my question at the top of the wall, written out on a sticky note. As I continued through the discernment process I would return to the wall and add to the notes. I used different colors by themes.

Some people prefer to do this electronically, others might want to keep a notebook or a journal. It is useful to have a dedicated space to return to, even if it is a computer file. I am a writer, so I think with words, but you could do this process with sketches, or images from other places, photographs or even music. Discernment playlists anyone? Throughout this book I will invite you to explore the concepts through questions and exercises. When I refer to those at the end of most chapters, my hope is that you will record what comes up for you in the space you have chosen.

I would often stand in front of the wall where I had my sticky notes from my discernment process. Over time, I would move them around. If they were no longer pertinent, I'd remove them. Others changed in importance. Sometimes these adjustments were small. At other times they really changed the discernment landscape. That's why I liked having them on a wall – I would see them whenever I walked downstairs, which was multiple times a day, and so they were always somewhere in my awareness.

Symbol

I work out of an office in my home. Outside my window is a hummingbird feeder. Birds show up throughout the day, tiny, gaily colored distractions dipping greedily into the yellow plastic flowers on the red plastic base.

I like symbolism. I like to create rituals and have objects around me that remind me of things that are important to me. I find it grounding. On my desk I have a small votive candle that I light when I am having an executive coaching session over video. My clients can't see the candle, but it reminds me that this is sacred work.

My husband travels often to New Mexico to see family. He brings me presents, often carved stone animals. On my desk are a small stone beaver and a blue stone giraffe decorated with leaves outlined in white. They signify the care and support I feel from my husband, as well as whimsy and play.

I have lots of plants in my house, and five in pots on my desk. I love to garden, and I find plants relaxing, and I enjoy caring for them. Occasionally I do hard things at my desk. Talking with people who are troubled, writing about bereavement, doing the dull but necessary chores attendant on self-employment. These touchstones of intention help me.

If the symbolic frame resonates for you, think of symbols that support you. If nothing comes to mind for you, sit with it as a warmup question and see what arises. You can try different things and see what fits.

Find your rhythm

Depending on how you learn and work, it can be useful to have a set time or schedule to do this work. Small regular slices of time are often more valuable than big chunks occasionally. But you may be in circumstances with little privacy or free time so the occasional chunks may be the only way you get to do this. Either way, decide what you want to do and can do and be intentional about it. You can use this book and do a page or chapter at a time. Or you can associate this process with another one, for example, if you do yoga at a studio twice a month, you may want to keep a notebook in your bag and commit to getting a cup of tea on the way to class and reading or writing for twenty minutes. Or your life may be so hectic right now that you just keep the book or your space close and do what you can. That's fine too.

Here is where I use the Ignatian suggestion to "rest where you find fruit." This means that if something is useful for you, keep doing it. If it is not useful for you, move on. This sounds simple, but in practice I have found it challenging. There's a narrative that growth and exploration is hard. Exercise until your muscles burn. Change is always terrifying and painful. Sometimes those things are true. But effort and struggle may be signs that this is just not the time for you to do whatever it is.

As you go through these exercises, you may find they are fruitful. You may think about a particular topic, write about it, spend time in your space making notes or drawing and find yourself talking about it with a friend. Or you may find that questions or topics fall flat for you. It doesn't seem like it's about you, or it just doesn't land. I want you to honor your resistance. If one of the principles of this work is that you know what is right for you, let's honor that throughout your discernment process.

I can tell the difference between honoring my resistance and procrastinating. But it took a while. Honoring my resistance, for me, happens when I recognize that resistance is coming from a deep part of me. It may be grief I don't want to engage with right now. Or it may be anger at a person or situation that I am still processing and not ready to metabolize. Or it may be a recognition that I've been doing lots of hard work recently and now is a time to rest. In that case I rest, and check in again about the next step in a week or two. I don't leave it forever. I put it away, but not out of sight.

Procrastination is shallower and crankier. It's a kind of emotional rash – I'm itchy and frustrated but I don't want to do anything to change that. I feel irritation with myself for not just doing the darn thing I keep putting off, which makes me put it off even more. I can become really entrenched in this place. And it doesn't get better until I do the thing.

When I first started a meditation practice it was almost impossible for me to sit still. A friend suggested I set a timer for three minutes. I could probably hold my breath for three minutes, so I could certainly mediate for three minutes.

So now, when I am procrastinating, I'll set a timer for three minutes and do the thing for three minutes. I can do almost anything for three minutes. Then after three minutes I check and see if I want to stop or keep going. A few three-minute sessions later, I've made a bit of headway and can keep going.

Keep that in mind if you run up against hesitation as you go through this work. Be curious about how you can understand the difference between resistance which you want to honor, and procrastination you want to push through. And when in doubt, be gentle with yourself.

Invitation to Explore

- What is your question for discernment? Do you feel like this is fully baked, or is it just in a draft version for now? Did it evolve as you worked through this chapter? How did it change?

- If you still don't know what you want to know, can you narrow it down? Usually, the questions are about
    - The kind of work you do or are planning to do, or the kind of work you want to do.
    - How to balance true work and econ, if those are not the same for you.
    - Who do you want in your life right now or what kind of people do you want around you? This could be a question about partnerships, family relationships, your work group, community, children, or where you live.
    - How do you want to show up in the world? You may be letting go of old narratives about who you are and what you are allowed to be or do.
    - How are you called to help others or to help the world? You may feel strongly about a particular problem in your community or the world and yet not know what you can or should be doing about it.

- Do any of these categories in the previous question stand out to you? Try writing or do creative work around them like sketching or making music. Return to them.

- Is the concept of work and econ relevant for you? What is your true work?

- Are there images or scenes in movies or books that resonate for you and evoke a sense of beginnings? Are there particular songs or pieces of music that inspire you? As I was discerning whether or not to write this book, I watched a movie where a woman was writing with a fountain pen in a notebook on a wooden desk in the sun. The window in front of the desk was open, and the sun was shining. The room was in a windmill on an island. The scene jumped out at me, I wanted to stop the movie and rewind so I could watch that part again and again. It lit me up. Which was useful information when it came to discerning if I should write this book at this time.

- What evokes beginnings in you?

- What makes you feel safe and ready to make something? It could be a place – your couch or a corner in your local coffee shop. It could be company – a dog at your feet or your child doing homework in the next room. It could be a type of music or a scented candle, a particular kind of tea. If you already make things in a place, think of doing this work in that place. If you love to bake, sit at your kitchen table. If you are an avid gardener, sit in your garden. As embodied beings, where we put our bodies and how they are supported as we discern is important.

- Write your question down, and put it somewhere prominently in your space, file or journal. You can always revise the question or the wording as we go along, but it's good to keep your question in your conscious awareness as much as possible.

If you like lists and ticking boxes, you can check off the first part of this process.

Your Thoughts

CHAPTER SIX

Your discernment map

I've seen waves of cultural narratives around work through my career. There was "hustle culture", where everyone was supposed to have a side hustle to make more money or break through in the arts. Much of the hustle was done on whatever social media platform was in vogue at the time, by people laboring for free in their spare time, for "exposure."

At one point the notion arose that you could manifest your reality through positive thinking. That may work for some, it's certainly never worked for me. I always felt like there was a carefully coiffed influencer looking at me from the side of their smoky eye and judging me for not understanding how to access the magical wavelength that would roll everything I wanted towards me, inexorably.

Because of this, I try to keep any work on discernment firmly grounded in reality. You can't make a decision without considering the practical needs of you and your family and the people who are dependent on you. I could have a story where I listened to my dream of being a writer and went to grad school for my Master of Fine Arts and carted my kids around the country from place to place while I wrote fiction and taught creative writing and was paid a pittance with bad health insurance as an untenured teaching assistant. But I moved around when I was a kid and I found it trying, so I didn't want to do that to my children. Another person might make the exact opposite choice and find that to be the right lifestyle for them and their children. The point is that we all need to consider what is supportive for the people who depend on us, as well as what is best for us. These beliefs may evolve when we look at the narratives society and our families taught us. But we need to start somewhere. The next section of the discernment process is to build a map of the facts that influence your life right now. Write them down. Keep one fact on one note, so you can move them around later.

The facts we're going to consider here are financial guardrails and practical obligations, what you know about yourself from your past work history, or education, your values and how those guide your work, and how to navigate a decision that impacts those values.

Let's start with the logistical guardrails impacting your decision. This is fairly factual: your finances and practical responsibilities. These facts may or may not be limiting, they may or may not impact any conclusions you come to regarding these facts in the future. Try not to judge, just list them. You can figure out later which ones to prioritize.

You want to focus on realities, like student loan debt and your mother's ill health, if you are one of her caregivers. What are the specifics of your current reality that you need to map out as you consider your decision? We will return to these realities again when we consider the narratives we carry, so for now just name them.

How will the decision you are making now impact your future? Ignatius, in a section about "Making a Correct and Good Choice of a Way of Life" (SE #184) suggests that we imagine what we might think of this decision looking back from our death bed. "This is to consider what procedure and norm of action I would wish to have followed in making the present choice if I were at the moment of death. I will guide myself by this and make my decision entirely in conformity with it." (SE #186)

Invitation to Explore

Which factors are impacting your decision? Below are a few suggestions, but you will have others. Note that many of these will be revisited in the section about stories we carry, since most of these are steeped in cultural narratives. I understand that some of these are complex and may seem daunting – considering my finances always feels like an emotional root canal to me. I've asked quite a few questions below, but I would suggest that it's more important to hit the high points and name them, rather than getting too in depth. Answering these in twenty minutes, to the best of your ability, may be more useful than spending hours going through in-depth examinations.

- **Consider finances**
    - How much money do you have coming in and what financial responsibilities do you have; child support, credit card debt, student loans? How would the decision you are considering impact your finances?

- Have you explored any options to mitigate any of these factors that might be limiting? For example, have you looked into programs to lessen student loan payments?
- What are your monthly living expenses? Will those change depending on your course of action? For example, will your living expenses be higher if you move to a new city for a job? Will you be able to pay your bills and accumulate and maintain at least a small savings account for emergencies?
- Are you confident that you are assessing your financial circumstances realistically? If not, can you think of resources that might help you better understand issues like budgeting or tax deductions? I've always found this kind of examination of my finances to be quite daunting, so I've gotten help from a financial advisor and helpful relatives and spent years developing my financial literacy.
- Are there future financial implications of choices you are making now? Student loans can be an investment in the future for some, and an impediment to future financial stability for others. Single women, especially, need to pay attention to saving for retirement.

- **Consider family**
  - What responsibilities do you feel you have toward family that impact your decision? You may have children, elderly parents who need help, or a family member with a disability. Those people's needs don't need to short circuit a discernment process that might include a move or change. But they need to be considered. Family can include a pet. I know of people who have waited to make a big change until a beloved older pet passed away.
  - If you are a caregiver, is there anyone else who can step in to help you?
  - If you are a parent, do you get the support and help you need from a co-parent? Are there any extended family or community resources that can help you?

- **Consider health**
    - Are there any health issues you are dealing with that impact your decision? For example, if you've just gone through chemotherapy and are building back your strength, that might impact your decision to move to another city in the next few months if most of the physical work of packing and unpacking would be your responsibility.
    - What kind of health care do you and your family need and how will you access it? People with health issues must consider access to healthcare facilities as well as health insurance coverage. Include mental health issues as well.

- **Consider your future**
    - How will this decision change your future options? Is this a time limited decision? A woman who is making a decision about whether or not to have a child and can't afford to have her eggs frozen has a window beyond which it will be difficult to get pregnant. Again, you don't have to decide anything now, but if there is a time limit in which to take an action, think about highlighting that.
    - What will you think when you are eighty about this decision? Will you regret not doing it?

- **Consider your safety**
    - Is there a risk to what you are considering? Is it a risk you are centering appropriately – neither exaggerating nor underestimating? Your race, sexuality, gender identity, and other factors can make certain situations or geographies unsafe or hostile. For example, if you work in the field of reproductive justice some locations are going to be dangerous for you. We need to be clear about any risks that we may encounter and take them into account.

As you come up with any practical considerations, write them down and capture them. You'll have an opportunity to revisit them later.

Your Thoughts

CHAPTER SEVEN

Values as navigational guides

My granddaughter Ruby really loves the Disney movie *Moana*. Which means I've watched it many, many times. Moana is a teenaged Polynesian girl who goes through adventures and ends up becoming a way finder, a skilled nautical navigator. A demigod named Maui teaches her how to navigate using the stars and other indicators in the natural world around her.

Wayfinding and navigation are part of the discernment journey as well. But instead of being guided by the stars, we're guided by our values, dreams and desires. In this chapter, we're going to consider ways in which your values impact life decisions you are considering.

"Then I will reflect on myself that I may reap some fruit." (SE #114)

Values

I've worked in and around advertising for most of my career. And one of the things I decided early on was that I would never work on marketing for a pharmaceutical company, or "pharma" as we called it. While there may, indeed, be one or two good "pharma" accounts, I don't personally know of any. I understand the degree to which pharmaceutical marketing and advertising has damaged the American healthcare system and led to an epidemic of deaths from opioids. This meant that when I was looking for a new job or considering who to partner with, I used this as a criteria. If an agency had pharma on their roster, I would pass them by. Other advertising people have accounts they won't work on; weapons, guns, alcohol.

What values do you have that impact your decisions? An obvious example would be a researcher who was committed to never working in a lab that experimented on animals. That would guide her choice of workplaces or research institutes.

The values that will guide you are the ones that come up quickly when you think about work and how you spend your time. You may have things you won't abide or circumstances that must be present. One person may choose to only work at organizations with policies that address climate change. Another may work at a vegetarian restaurant rather than a steak house because he is a vegan.

Clearly, not everyone has the privilege of being able to make these kinds of choices. I still have found it useful to know what they are, because I can have the goal of being able to align my personal values with where I work and what I do in the future.

Meaning

I'm the kind of person who needs meaning in her work. It's very difficult for me to do a job that doesn't mean something to me. Even when I was working in the worst advertising jobs, I focused on the fact that I was using income from the job to support my children. I like the saying that if you don't like your job, like why you do your job. Some people need meaning in their work, others don't, and many of us can do the mental gymnastics I did to invent meaning where there isn't any. Know which one you are.

I have a number of friends who intentionally choose work that helps the world through medicine, non-profits, advocacy or public policy. I can't imagine them being happy doing something else, even though their jobs are often demanding and don't pay as well as for-profit jobs.

Only you can decide how much meaning you need in your work, and which values you want to use to guide you. If you're not in a space where this resonates, that's fine as well. When I was younger and broke, I just wanted a job where I could make enough money doing anything legal to keep my electricity from being shut off. I have often found meaning outside of my work, participating in community in a way that was meaningful to me when my work was meaningless. Our vegan friend might have to work at a steakhouse because it's the only job he can get, and he may choose to work at an animal shelter a few times a month to stay connected to his values.

First, decide if meaning is important to you and if that impacts your decision. Then consider what values are important enough to you that they need to be taken into account in this discernment process. Use a different color or design for the notes where you write your values. They might not all be pertinent to your specific question, but add them anyway.

Invitation to explore

- On a scale of 1 to 10, how much meaning do you need in your job? Without judgement, think about where you would fall on a continuum that goes from a 1 where you don't need meaning in your job, it's strictly econ, to a 10, where you have a deep need to do work which helps others, the world, or a specific cause.

- What are the most pressing political, social or environmental issues for you? Are there any implications regarding those issues that might impact your decision?

- Are there any ethical mandatories for you? "I must or must not work in an environment where . . ."

- Do you think it is better for you to work in a for-profit or nonprofit workplace? Are there ethical guidelines for you around for-profit work?

- Do you have a religious tradition or belief system with practices or teachings that impact your vocational choices?

- Can you think of a person who was ethical about their work in a way you respect? It could be a family member, someone in your community or a historical figure. What do you admire about this person and their choices? Does this give you any additional perspective about your values?

- Once you have written down these values, can you sort them? Are there ones that are more important than others? Are any of them in conflict with one another? For example, if you want to impact government policy on healthcare in a significant way but believe large corporations and the government work in unethical ways, those values could potentially be in conflict with one another, and you will need to sort out which value takes priority. We will explore this more in the next chapter.

- Does this exercise impact your decision or reframe the question you are asking? Are there any other implications that arise for you?

Your Thoughts

CHAPTER EIGHT

Pick a Side

What do you do if one of your values is in conflict with your work?

Ignatius has an exercise called A Mediation on Two Standards (SE #136). By standards, he means a flag or banner. Ever the soldier, he invites us to imagine that there are two armies going into battle. Each army has a flag, a standard or banner unfurled above the troops riding into battle. One army is led by Jesus. The other army is led by Lucifer. It might be easier to think of good versus evil here.

In the Two Standards, Ignatius says we should ask for "knowledge of the deceits of the rebel chief and help to guard myself against them; and also to ask for a knowledge of the true life exemplified in the sovereign and true Commander, and the grace to imitate Him." (SE #139)

I have to admit that this is one of my favorite meditations in the Exercises. It's so dramatic. Soldiers on horseback, riding in two groups toward conflict, each led by a powerful figure, the banners snapping in the wind overhead.

Sometimes, a discernment process about work requires us to make a decision about what side we're on. There are good and bad jobs, ethical and unethical projects. You know what your values and beliefs are. A job that violates your beliefs brings you to the question of how much your beliefs actually guide you. What are the lies we tell ourselves, the "deceits" that come from our greed or fear? Do we understand what our true work is, is it a life grounded in what is best and truest for us? Or have we been deceived by what other people told us our life should be?

I imagine that when Purdue Pharma, owned by the Sackler family was planning on flooding the market with advertising touting how well OxyContin controlled pain, there were individuals involved in that process who knew it was problematic. Maybe it was a scientist who realized that Oxy was much more addictive than the marketing let on. Maybe it was a consultant who woke up in the middle of the night wondering if her expertise and knowledge was best used to help the Sacklers make more millions at the risk of thousands becoming addicted to pain pills. Maybe it was the lawyers who have helped the Sackler family avoid ongoing lawsuits over their involvement in the deaths of over 100,00 Americans every year, according to NPR[1].

Each person in that situation made a choice. Where were they going to use their talents? To keep the Sacklers one of the wealthiest families in the world? Or to work to hold them accountable for what they wrought? Each person chose which banner they were going to fight under, which side they were going to work to bring to victory.

One of the reasons I like this meditation is that I like binaries and clear-cut dualities. I long for black and white answers. But I know that's not how spirituality works. As my spiritual director recently reminded me, each of our skills, talents and desires can have a light side and a shadow side. Ambition can be positive, helping someone persevere through a difficult training program, for example. Ambition can also be negative if it causes someone to cheat on a certification exam, or steal another's work and claim it as their own. I would have a different opinion of that consultant who was helping the Sacklers if I knew that her job was helping her pay for expensive medical treatment for a sick child. In her conflict between providing for a loved one with significant medical issues and working for a company she thought was bad, I would understand her choosing to do a job she didn't think was ethical to keep her kid alive.

The Ignatian term "discernment of spirits" can be useful here. Sometimes we have to discern between conflicting values, needs, desires and responsibilities. When I'm considering a particular course of action, where is there conflict? What are the roots of the conflict? In fear or greed? Or a desire to help or be heard? Where are the battle lines? Which specific elements are in opposition? Outlining what exactly the conflict is can be helpful.

If I think of it like sound, the noise when I'm being drawn to the shadow side is catchy but discordant, a little too loud, at a frequency that irritates after a while. It's the emotional equivalent to drinking too much coffee, a jittery hyper focus. When I'm drawn to the positive side, it's calmer, a more sustained interest, engaging but not overstimulating, like, for me, listening to Yo Yo Ma play Bach.

Here's an example from my life. At the beginning of the pandemic, almost all my clients cancelled their contracts. Fear of the financial repercussions of the global pandemic caused many corporations to cut back on any consulting,

1 Brian Mann, Aneri Pattani, Carrie Feibel, "Supreme Court overturns opioid settlement with Purdue Pharma that shielded Sacklers" https://www.npr.org/sections/shots-health-news/2024/06/29/nx-s1-5021798/supreme-court-overturns-opioid-settlement-with-purdue-pharma-that-shielded-sacklerssupreme-court-overturns-sackler-settlement-delaying-funds-meant-for-communities-battling-opioids

training, or executive coaching, which is what I did. One of my clients offered me a job as a part time Chief Marketing Officer. It wasn't the first time they had offered me this job. I had turned it down before, after a discernment process. When I thought it through and used these tools, the answer was a clear no. I didn't want to work in advertising anymore. But this time, early in the pandemic, I said yes. I didn't discern, I just jumped, because I was afraid of running out of money, driven by fear and scarcity.

The company itself was not a force for darkness. It was just an ad agency. There were good people, and less skillful people. I liked and respected the woman who was my boss. I loved the team of women I worked with, and I was able to hire a good friend to start an interesting project. But for me, I chose the wrong banner to fight under. The work was stressful and demanding. The global reach of the organization meant I had conference calls from early morning to late evening. Like many organizations, there was sexism and racism. When I saw it, I spoke up about it. That didn't endear me to anyone, but there wasn't any change. I was so stressed out from my job I started getting sick. What was supposed to be econ, a way to pay the bills, metastasized into a job that took over my life and damaged my spirit.

I was really infatuated with the role and the money. When the CEO would introduce me as the CMO my heart gave a little skip, reacting to the title like I'd just seen someone I had a crush on. Every time my paycheck hit the bank, I saw the number and felt that little internal dance of success. I was greedy for the title and the cash.

That's often how these bad choices begin. The "chief of all the enemy in the vast plain about Babylon" (SE #140) tempted me to "covet riches (as Satan himself is accustomed to do in most cases) that they may more easily attain the empty honors of this world . . ." (SE # 142) I was hooked on the money. I was able to fix up my house in a way that I hadn't been able to afford in the many years I'd lived there. New roof, new siding and paint, two remodeled bathrooms. When they pulled up the floor in the downstairs bathroom the wood was rotted, and they said if I'd waited much longer the toilet would have fallen through into the basement.

It's a good thing, I told myself, to have the money to fix up the house, finally. It doesn't matter that I'm not sleeping well, my body is rebelling, and I'm constantly anxious and exhausted. The "honors" of being CMO were absolutely "empty honors", and I was moving away from anything that felt like my "true life." My family and friends saw the change in me. I became more stressed, irritable. People who love me suggested I should leave the job, it wasn't worth it, but I resisted. It took me a long time to finally leave, to walk away, exhausted and dirty, battle worn.

Hopefully, your work decisions will be between different levels of good and you won't have to choose which banner you're fighting under. But if you want to be intentional about your work, and you've identified your moral values and framework about work, you might have to choose.

The shadow-side jobs often pay the most money, offer the most access to status and power. I revved up my engine of self-justification and told myself I was supporting my family, I could help change the system from the inside, build wealth for future generations, build a wall against illness or disaster. At what cost? To the world, to my family, or my health and well-being?

How do we know?

At the time, I didn't see the decision to be the CMO as a moral choice. I didn't think of the Two Standards at all. It was only in retrospect that I recognized the choice I had made.

How do you know if you're in a Two Standards situation? At the beginning of this meditation, Ignatius refers to "Lucifer, the deadly enemy of our human nature." (SE #136) If one of your choices works in opposition to your human nature, it might be the wrong choice. Our human nature needs community, meaning, rest, play, stories, connection, sleep, time in the outdoors. Many jobs work in opposition to our human nature. Jobs that force us to return to work days after the death of a loved one. Or a job that makes someone return to work with a body not yet healed from childbirth.

Does your work support your human nature or oppose it? The "deadly" enemy of our human nature could be the kind of toll stress and the pressures of capitalism can put on our bodies. Every few years, a leading light in the advertising world will be written up in an obituary. Often these are younger people, in their thirties, forties or fifties. They are highflyers, traveling extensively in a global role, moving up corporate ladders that don't elevate people who just work nine to five. I always wonder, would they have died that young if they had a lower stress position working fewer hours?

I'm not a big one for regrets, but I wish I'd worked different jobs, I wish I had worked less and traveled less. I wish I'd been home more with my children when they were young. I had that ignorant confidence that there would be all sorts of time, that I'd have a future with my son RJ where he'd finish high school, go to college, find a career, maybe get married and have a couple of kids. All the things his friends, some who are still my friends, are doing with their lives now. He died at nineteen. I chose the wrong side. Again and again.

Of course, I'm grateful that my kids didn't want for food, clothing or health care once I established my career. I'm grateful that I was able to buy a house in the olden days, decades ago, when a single mom could find an affordable place thirty minutes outside of Seattle. And I appreciate that I worked in jobs where I was competent, sometimes talented, and I met wonderful people. But I am careful now, knowing I am so susceptible to the blandishments of fame and financial security, to understand in any discernment process what sides are in conflict, and which banner I want to stand under.

Invitation to explore:

- Do you have a weak spot in decision making? What are your inordinate attachments? Are you greedy for power? Money? Influence? Fame?

- If you were a character in a graphic novel and a demon was tempting you, what would the demon use? Superman was weakened by Kryptonite – what's your Kryptonite? It is entirely possible that you don't have a weak spot or temptation, this might not apply to you. I'm the drunk, not the saint. I'm a festival of inordinate attachments.

- Have you or someone you know ever been in a situation where you had to choose between a good and a bad choice? What did you or your friend choose? How did that work out?

- Is there anything in this Meditation on Two Standards that resonates with you? What do you think the flags of the good/light or the bad/shadow sides look like?

- Think of one of your skills. It could also be a dream or desire. Can you think of a light aspect as well and shadow aspect of how that might show up in your life? Do you have any experience of this happening to you before?

- In considering your work history, are there any decisions you made or jobs you took that you now realize were in opposition to your human nature?

- What does it mean for you to have your work support your human nature? How can you make that personal for you?

- Does this evoke any new insights that are pertinent to your discernment question?

Your Thoughts

CHAPTER NINE

Knowing yourself

Once, when I worked at a small agency, I had an office adjacent to an open space where most of the other people worked. One of the men that worked there liked to listen to music when he worked. He preferred his music over the speakers rather than headphones. I didn't mind his choice of music, but I minded the noise. I don't listen to music when I work. I find it really distracting. He felt like he needed music to work, and that I was being a jerk when I asked him to listen on headphones. He thought I was depriving the team of the opportunity to share his music over the office speakers. I thought he was depriving us of the opportunity for silence, and the ability to control our own aural environment.

There are people who like noise, others who prefer silence. Understanding your preferences in a work environment and culture can be useful in making a decision. If you are discerning a question about something else, perhaps connected to relationships, then you can reframe this to consider what you know about yourself in relationship, for example.

What do you know about yourself that you need to keep in mind as you make this decision? Let's start with the practicalities of work and the working environment. Then we'll look at our skills, challenges and the kind of people with whom we like to work.

We all have certain ways we prefer to work and individual strengths and weaknesses. Sometimes we overlook these or carry an idealized version of what we could or should be. It can be helpful to take stock of what we know about ourselves and how we work and to stay grounded in that reality as we discern what kind of work we want to do.

In many spiritual traditions, an understanding of where we lack skill and a readiness to admit that to a trusted elder or friend and accept responsibility is a key part of developing spiritual maturity. Step Four in the Twelve Steps is "Made a searching and fearless moral inventory of ourselves." Step Five is "Admitted to God, to ourselves and to another human being the exact nature of our wrongs." (BB p. 59). The First Week of the Spiritual Exercises is about understanding our "sins" with multiple "examination(s) of conscience." It amuses me that both Ignatius and Wilson used a chart format for cataloging and documenting these respective lists.

Here we're going to try to inventory our work behaviors, our skills and challenges. We're going to include the positive as well as the less skillful traits and tendencies, because they are all instructive.

I'll start. I am easily bored. I like variety and risk at work. It took me a long time to admit this because I wanted to be someone who was more solid and dependable, a reliable workhorse.

When I started working in advertising, I was doing new business; getting new clients, usually through a pitch process that was as labor intensive and stressful as putting on a theatrical performance. When we were working on a pitch I was energized and excited. I could work long hours, sometimes through the night. My brain felt like it was working faster and more efficiently. I drank vats of coffee and smoked a lot of cigarettes. I loved the camaraderie with the rest of the team who worked on the pitch. And I loved when we did creative work, because I could be more involved in the actual creative process than I normally was.

But after the pitch was finished, even if we won, I would crash. I'd come to work and look at my computer and feel paralyzed with boredom. This was the time I thought I would be cleaning up my files, returning and organizing emails, finishing up expense reports, researching new prospects to approach. In my mind, that's who I wanted to be. In reality, it took all the willpower I had to stay at my desk on those days. While a ten-hour day working a pitch whizzed by, in the post-pitch ennui I often thought the clock on my computer was broken because there was no possible way it was still morning, let alone 9:17 am. When I admitted to myself that I like a regular stream of different kinds of projects and that I don't do well with down time or time spent on details like projections or sales reports, it made making decisions about work easier.

I often had conflicts with my supervisors. If I was working for someone who was a good boss, and better than I was in certain areas, I was loyal and hard working. If I was working for another mediocre white guy who mansplained my own job to me, I would be surly, churlish and generally difficult. I was such a high performer that I didn't think I had to concern myself with the politics at work. Which meant that throughout my twenties and thirties and even into my forties I was highly productive and a pain in the ass for many of my bosses.

Now I work for myself, and have for almost a decade. I choose my clients carefully, and work with people I respect and appreciate who usually return the favor. I pay someone else to do my bookkeeping and accounting, and I have a wide range of work I can do each day, depending on my frame of mind, but there is always variety.

How can we be realistic in our assessment of what we are like at work? Humility.

Humility is a concept that is often misunderstood, but to me it just means being accurate in my self-assessment and thinking of myself less often. The more humility we can bring to our understanding of both our strengths and weaknesses at work, the better. C.S. Lewis writes that humility is not about negating or disowning our strengths and abilities or "clever men trying to believe that they are fools." That, he goes on, "may, in some cases be manifest nonsense."[1] Rather, it is understanding who and what we are realistically.

In Twelve Step programs there is a whole step about humility. Step Seven says "Humbly asked Him to remove our shortcomings" (BB p.59) the "Him" in this case referring to the Divine or our Higher Power. The word "humbly" was troublesome. When writing more about Step Seven in the later book *The Twelve Steps and Twelve Traditions,* Wilson wrote "Humility, as a word and as an ideal, has a very bad time of it in our world. Not only is the idea misunderstood; the word itself is often intensely disliked." (12x12 p. 70)

Staying grounded in humility as much as we can, let's review our strengths and challenges as we know them from our experience working. If you have little work experience or aren't sure, consider your strengths and weaknesses at school or in any community organization from choir to sports teams to a youth group. If that's not relevant, then the childhood cues we will review in our next chapter can be a guide.

Skills and Superpowers

Make a list of what you do well at work. If you don't have much work experience, make a list of what you do well, period. Consider everything, even if it isn't valued by society. Put your art in there, your hobbies, your passions. Put in interpersonal skills. Do people tell you their problems? Are you a great listener? Do kids gravitate towards you at any family gathering? Are you really good with elders?

If you know your way around social media and are great at creating for any of those platforms, that would be a useful skill for marketing. If you're naturally

[1] jhttps://www.npr.org/2023/04/13/1168961388/pew-earnings-gender-wage-gap-housework-chores-child-care

inclined to ask questions and generally curious, that could be especially useful for investigative work from journalism to law enforcement.

There are skills and talents and then there are superpowers. Superpowers are skills or talents that are unusual, exceptional or especially in demand. I've noticed in my work as an executive coach that many women don't understand that their unique skills are unique or a skill. They have superpowers that don't even make it onto their list of skills. "Can't everyone do that?" is often the response when I point out a superpower. No, everyone cannot do that. We need to recognize our superpowers as superpowers.

When you look back at your work experience, are there jobs or projects where something came easily to you that seemed challenging for others? Did you ever become the "go-to" person for a particular skill for a team? I was often the go-to person when it came to dealing with difficult leaders. "Stephanie can talk to him" became a refrain at jobs where a challenging leader was making bad business decisions. Even the difficult leaders themselves realized that I could be counted on to tell them the unvarnished truth. At one job, a leader who was prone to rash, bad decisions agreed to what we called a red flag process. If he made a bad decision, I could throw a red flag and he'd have to listen to my argument. I couldn't make him to change his mind – he owned the company – but I could get him to listen.

The red flag was a piece of red cloth wrapped around a tennis ball, with enough excess cloth to make a tail like a comet. It was kept in the open office space in the center of the ad agency, and when I walked over to pick it up, everyone stopped working to watch me. I would pick up the red flag, walk into the boss's office and throw it down on his desk. Everyone was watching at this point, and then I'd tell him what I thought.

I didn't enjoy that role, but I realized that it was a superpower, the ability to challenge a leader with clarity and directness while still being professional. I now have clients who pay me to do exactly that because good leaders need that kind of unvarnished naming of reality and not everyone has the capacity, skills or interest to do that.

When you have unique skills that are not aligned with capitalism or white supremacy, they may be discounted by others. Reclaim them. The cross-cultural competence of someone who is an immigrant or who was raised by immigrants and is bilingual or multilingual is incredibly valuable, not just in cross cultural work environments but in any work environment where different people work together – which is all work environments. The ability to understand the strengths and weaknesses of a team and how to get them to pull together is a leadership skill. If you have two or more kids, or have ever coached a child's sports team, you probably already know how to do that.

Often, we can't see our own superpowers and we need our friends and family as a guide to show us the special or quirky things they see that we need to notice for ourselves. If you are the one who always pulls together parties and social events and helps with your friends' weddings, that's a skill for event organizing.

My friend Nayda was a public defender in Los Angeles, and she came into a meeting with a client, a young man who had been arrested, again, for tagging a building. She opened up the file with the pictures of his graffiti.

"You know what I'm looking at here?" she said. He shook his head. "A portfolio," she said, "this is a portfolio of your artwork."

We all could use a Nayda to name or reframe our strengths when we can't see them or when they have been devalued by others.

This might take you a while. This section may be especially important to someone who is early in their career and discerning what kind of work they want to do, or someone who is leaving one career to begin another. If that describes your discernment process, take your time here. Enlist the help of elders, family or friends with jobs you like to review your list of skills and see which might be superpowers.

Challenges

Once you've gotten your list of skills and superpowers, let's look at your challenge areas. I use the word challenge because there are things that may be challenging to navigate in certain work situations or cultures, not because they are a reflection of some personal shortcoming on your part, but because the workplace is racist or sexist or rife with dysfunction. In other cases, we have habits or responses which aren't helpful and are our responsibility to address.

Write down challenges you've had in work or school. My list would include trouble with authority figures. That isn't always negative, but it has gotten me in trouble in hierarchical male dominated corporate workplaces where bosses didn't know how to manage me effectively. I'm not good at some very detail-oriented tasks but I'm good at seeing the big picture and how systems work together. But my lack of attention to detail can be – and has been – challenging.

This list may not be long. It also may include environmental challenges, like my preference for silence. I'm deeply introverted and prefer to work alone for much of the day, but I love being part of a team and working toward a shared goal. As long as I don't have to be with them all the time. If you need any special accommodations in how or where you work, these should be noted, without judgement, as something to consider.

Once you have your list of any challenges, try to extrapolate any implications. What does this mean about you and what jobs might suit you? For me, I need to be in a fast-paced environment with lots of variety where I can be creative, and I don't have to deal with lots of detail or process.

If you, like me, have work experience behind you and know of specific personal challenge areas that you would like to address, it can be good to capture those here. Clearly, most of us have areas where we could improve. A key leadership skill is understanding your weaknesses and strengths and being strategic in addressing them. Some work on skills in executive coaching or through reading and education. Others may try to mitigate their weaknesses by having staff or co-workers who are strong where they are weak, like having a person on their team who loves networking and public speaking if that's not something they enjoy or tolerate well. If you're in a circumstance where you are considering changing jobs or careers, could this also be an opportunity to start new practices or build more skill in certain areas?

One note on feedback. Often, the feedback you are given in school or at work reflects the lens the feedback giver is wearing. Which means that not all feedback is going to be useful to you in your discernment process. If you're part of a marginalized community, the way supervisors or instructors view your performance or suitability for a position may say more about their limitations than your abilities.

On the other side, those of us with lots of privilege can take credit for accomplishments that are actually an extension of our privilege rather than something we did on our own.

If you have a guide or trusted friend who you are checking in with during this process, this is an especially good place to get their feedback on your list of skills, superpowers and challenges to validate if you are being accurate and compassionate with yourself.

People

What kind of people do you enjoy spending time with at work or in your personal life?

My daughter Emma is a nurse. She's worked in Emergency Rooms, ICUs and surgical centers. She gets along well with most nurses, many of her friends are in the medical field. At one party at my house with her friends, I looked around and realized there were paramedics, firefighters, ER nurses and ICU nurses and thought, well, if anyone were going to have a heart attack, this would be the place to do it. She and her friends are the people who run in when everyone is running out. They are brave and resourceful and ready for anything.

On the other hand, caregivers, like many of us, don't always consider their own well-being and can get caught up tending to others and neglect their own needs.

Most groups of people who are attracted to similar careers share traits or general approaches to life. The point is not to engage in stereotyping but to understand if there are certain environments that appeal to you where you would be a good personality fit with the other people who work there. A group of software developers is going to be very different from a group of people who work in and around the theater. If you are considering a job or career where you work in a group, team or community – which is most jobs, let's face it – you want to mesh with the group you're in as much as possible. You may decide to be part of a group that has more people of your race or gender. You may realize you need to be part of a community that is committed to social justice or political change or spiritual practice. The list is endless but it's good to consider the people who will be around you as part of your team or the community you are serving when you are thinking about work.

Invitation to Explore:

- How do you physically like to work? Do you like music and noise, or do you prefer quiet? Can you work for long stretches at one task, or do you need variety and regular shifts in pace?

- How much supervision do you prefer? Total freedom and self-direction or a clear understanding of what you need to do and how success will be measured?

- Make a list of your skills. Which of these are superpowers?

- Make a list of challenges you have at work. Think of situations where the way you are or who you are is difficult for systems to manage. Also consider patterns where you could be more skillful.

- What do you enjoy most about work?

- What is your least favorite thing?

- Are you detail oriented? Is it interesting or satisfying for you to be into details and getting everything organized?

- Do you like having people around and working in groups that develop work or ideas together? Or do you prefer to work alone and reconnect with others to report out? Or do you want to be entirely alone?

- How important is it for you to be able to work from home all or part of the time? How important is it for you to be able to be in an office or shared workspace all or part of the time? What is the optimal balance of those for you?

- How physically active do you want to be at work? Do you like desk jobs, or do you need something where you are moving around? Do you want to work outside in nature, or work in circumstances where you travel about, like a residential plumber or electrician?

- Do you prefer working with your hands, your brain or both?

- How much do you want to deal with the public in your job?

- How much travel are you interested in doing for a job?

- What kind of work would you do even if you didn't get paid for it? Hobbies or passions can be a good guide in discernment, whether you love animals, board games, fly fishing or playing the cello.

- What was your favorite job? What does that tell you about how you like to work?

- What was your least favorite job, or task/s at a job? What does that tell you?

- Have you gotten consistent feedback in school or work settings about strengths or weaknesses? Which of those do you consider to be valid?

- Review your list of skills and potential superpowers. Then run it by someone you trust. Ask them if there is anything that is missing. If you have an idea of what kind of field you'd like to be in, see if you can find someone in your community who is in that field. Show them the list and see what they think. I can identify superpowers for advertising that someone who hadn't been in advertising might miss.

- If you find the exercise of identifying your challenges or skills to be inordinately difficult, or if you find yourself ruminating or feeling distress, consider pausing and returning to this after you have read the chapter on The Inner Community.

- Did anything arise here that's pertinent to your discernment question? Try to capture any findings in the space you are using.

Your Thoughts

CHAPTER TEN

Clues from childhood

Often, what we are called to do is something that showed up for us when we were children. Looking back at your childhood or youth can offer clues. If you have older relatives or people in your community who knew you when you were a child, they may have insights or stories that could help you with this.

My daughter was interested in medicine when she was little. As an elementary school student, she wanted the book Gray's Anatomy, the actual anatomy book, with drawings. I remembered this, although she didn't, so I wasn't surprised when she became a nurse.

I always loved writing. My earliest memory is of learning how to write. I have almost no memories of anything that happened to me before I started school, but I remember learning how to write. I was by myself, at home, writing on a piece of paper on a small table. I was using a pencil, and I was writing with my left hand, and I wrote my first name. I was taught in school to write with my right hand, and I think it's interesting that I remember starting out left-handed, that even something as basic as handedness was forced on me.

I remember learning how to read, that moment when every billboard and scrap of paper sprang into sound in my head. I could disappear into a book for hours and emerge, slightly disoriented and sated. It was escape, safety, engagement and it stimulated my imagination to experience these fictional other lives.

What did you dream about when you were a kid? I always wanted to be a writer and I always wanted to be famous. I remember being in elementary school and walking on a hot summer day up the hill to my house, participating in an imaginary interview. I was waving my hands and talking out loud, very seriously considering every answer I was giving to the imaginary audience. I was a famous writer, and I was talking about my writing with the imaginary journalist. I must have walked up that hill hundreds of times and I was having that daydream almost every time. I never wanted to be a doctor or nurse, I never played with dolls or planned a future wedding, I just dreamed about writing books and being interviewed about my great work.

Other cues have less of a straight line, but are useful for us to note. When I was a kid, I became obsessed with Sherlock Holmes. I found this odd, flowered hat that looked like the deerstalker hat that Holmes wore – except in a flower pattern – and I wore it every day to school for a year. I read and reread every Holmes story, and everything I could find about Holmes.

I still enjoy detective fiction and read quite a bit of it. But I also think I recognized my own patterns in Holmes. He gets bored easily, and doesn't do well if his mind isn't engaged – that was why he started using drugs. He likes stimulants, cocaine, tobacco. He loved disguises and often fooled Dr. Watson by appearing in convincing makeup. I'm a recovering alcoholic, and am prone to follow the dictum "if a little is good, more is better." I like to work alone, sometimes in a psychological disguise. Art is important to me to make sense of my world. Holmes withdrew with his violin and lots of pipe tobacco when sorting out a thorny case. I used to write fiction with a pack of American Spirits and an ashtray next to me and would look over in surprise to find the ashtray overflowing and the box of cigarettes empty. Holmes is a competent reclusive weirdo. Which is kind of how I think of myself sometimes.

Mary Virginia is my oldest friend. We met when we were twelve and have been friends ever since. For most of our lives we've spoken on the phone every day. We used to write each other letters, back in the days when people wrote letters to each other. By hand. We've kept each other's letters and will reread them sometimes, she'll send me a copy of something I wrote when we were twenty, or I'll send her something that presaged where we ended up later in our lives.

When we were in middle school together, Mary Virginia and I used to do skits in Social Studies class about current affairs. I read everything I could get my hands on, including newspapers and magazines about politics. Our teacher, Mr. Shoemaker, was indulgent and would let us do a skit in the first few minutes of class. We didn't take up much time and, looking back, I realize we were funny. Mary Virginia and I both spend time on stages now. The stages are different – we're doing trainings and teaching people what we know. But the question of how we can take something potentially dry and bring it to life for others is one we continue to ask a half a century later, in two completely different fields.

For some of us, thinking of our youth and childhood is painful or distressing. Like anything in this process, if this doesn't resonate for you, skip it. But even challenging childhoods may have moments of connection. A beloved pet. A spot in nature where you felt calm and safe as you looked at the bugs skimming the top of the water. The satisfaction of building a model airplane, or writing a piece of code, or throwing a ball or running fast. I read to escape, others use television or movies or comic books. Many artists go on to make more of the very work they turned to for solace, like novels, movies or comic books.

For those of us who are around young children, this awareness that childhood interests can hint at a calling may dignify what children are drawn to, so we don't discount it as "child's play." What if it is practice for a future passion?

My mother insisted that women should be able to play the piano, so my sister and I had to take piano lessons. I was not talented or inclined to play piano. I wanted to play the drums, which was out of the question. Not surprisingly, I had a son who loved to play the drums. And I loved to listen. I love percussion of all kinds. I have pictures of my granddaughter as a baby clanking toys together with that same delight in percussion. Her father, my son in law, is a musician, and if she is drawn to music when she's older, I'll tell her the story of her making sound before she could walk, and show her the picture her father took of her curled up inside his silent bass drum, cozy.

Invitation to Explore

- What are happy memories from your childhood? Think particularly of memories where you were doing something; riding your bike outside, or staging a play in a neighbor's garage or helping your father cook or chasing fireflies at night around your yard.

- What did you do well as a child? Often in groups children are known for something. My sister ran fast and could draw well. Mary Virginia was a good actress. What did you do well, or feel drawn to do?

- Were their chores or household duties that you enjoyed? Did you love to help the adults garden or build things or care for animals?

- What was your relationship to the outdoors, nature, or the seasons? Were you in a city and not exposed to much open space? Or did you live on a farm? Were you drawn to a specific type of nature, the woods, or lakes or the ocean, mountains or the desert?

- Could you concentrate for long periods of time on a project or were you quick to move on?

- Was there something you wanted to do that you didn't get a chance to do as a child or young person? Does that still call to you?

- Were there jobs or activities that someone in your family did that were appealing to you? Do you have memories of a family member painting or knitting or cooking or laying bricks, the kind of memories that can be highlighted with a sense memory or the shimmer of pleasure?

- If you have older relatives or family friends who knew you when you were a child, do they have any memories of what you were like as a child that could reflect on your discernment question? What did you like to do? What was your temperament? Consider what that brings up for you. Does it seem accurate?

- If you have children, grandchildren or other young family members, does/did being around them when they are/were small evoke memories for you of your childhood? Is there anything that they do or did that reminds you of you when you were little?

- Are there any implications from your childhood interests or behaviors that relate to the decision you are currently considering?

Meditation with your senses

You could also enter into a memory or a recollection of something that interested or engaged you when you were a child. Think of doing something that you enjoyed as a child. Put yourself in the place where you did that thing. Then engage your senses. What do you see? Smell? What tactile information is available to your hands or feet, what do you touch? Are you alone? If not, who are you with? Is it warm? Cold? Temperate? If you are outside, what season is it? When you are grounded in the physical sense memories, consider what your emotional memories are. Do you feel calm or excited? Happy or peaceful? How do those emotions show up in your body? Do you enjoy being alone or are you appreciating a connection with the person or animal you are with? What comes up for you in this meditation?

Consider any implications for your discernment question and capture any information in the space you are using.

Your Thoughts

CHAPTER ELEVEN

The Inner Community

Part of understanding yourself in this discernment process is knowing if you are accurately assessing your strengths and weaknesses. Sometimes we over or underestimate our abilities. Privilege can cause us to inflate our abilities, thinking that we are naturally talented or good at business when, in fact, we succeeded because we inherited opportunities or wealth or both. Others are so filled with self-doubt they discount their real skills and accomplishments.

There's even a psychological term for it. The Dunning-Kruger effect is when a person with low skill overestimates their abilities and a person with high skill underestimates their abilities.

Think of a man who sings moderately well in his church choir yet believes he has recording star talent. Or the poet who is quite skilled, but compares herself to established poets and thinks she's terrible.

Both of them lack perspective. They can't assess the reality of their talents and abilities. Imagine the church singer who overestimates his talent and uproots his life to move to New York with the dream of being a star and getting a record deal. Had he been accurate in his self-assessment, he might have done something less radical. On the other hand, the talented poet, convinced she's no good, might not pursue the fellowships, education, or publication opportunities for which she is qualified because she lacks a realistic understanding of her skills.

Of course, using the Dunning-Kruger model, most of us want to be the talented one who doesn't understand how great her talent actually is. And yet I think we all can have biases that cause us to under or overestimate our talents. Sometimes we can overestimate in one area and underestimate in another.

I think I'm a great baker, but I'm not. The reality is I'm the only one in my family who likes to bake, and my family is vocal in appreciation of anything home cooked. But when I go to a bakery or restaurant and taste the creations of a pastry chef, I realize I'm just an average home baker.

What voices come up in your head when you consider your skills, abilities or advantages in life? I have a whole Greek chorus in my head that has an ongoing commentary on everything I think or do. Do you?

The voices aren't actually voices I hear, rather they are ongoing contributions from characters who seem to live in my head. Some of those characters are repeating things I heard before, from unskillful or unkind people I've known in my past. Others are trying to be helpful by suggesting coping mechanisms that no longer serve, or sounding alarms that aren't justified.

The one who says I don't deserve it. I don't deserve anything, apparently, according to this one.

The one who says I'm going to lose everyone I care about.

The one who says it's probably better not to try so I don't get disappointed.

"You're too much" was a refrain I heard quite a bit in my life, and I've internalized that.

It helps to listen to these voices during the discernment process, if only to understand which ones to let go.

Many of the messages I hear are from stories I was told, which we'll explore more in the next section. When we are told something often as a child we can believe it, like the "sickly" child who grows up to find he's strong enough to enjoy a wide range of physical activities he was told he was too weak to pursue. Other times our fears or insecurities can create a distorted view of potential risks that aren't really that risky. Sometimes recovering alcoholics talk about their minds, where these voices shout and spit, as a bad neighborhood, or an "itty bitty shitty committee."

But I don't want to be at war with those different voices in my head. I prefer to think of them as members of a community. My spiritual director calls them my "inner community." We don't always like or appreciate everyone in a community. But we need to put up with them, make peace with them. I like the idea that those differing voices and perspectives in my own mind are members of my inner community.

When I was a child, there was a man who went to the same Mass we did every Sunday. He was tall and thin with dark hair, and he vibrated with energy. Often, he would bang his fists together during Mass. He did something with his fingers to create a surface that made as much noise as a clap, even though his fists were clenched. He could clap very fast. It was hard to tell what agitated him, but sometimes he would clap loud and long. And other times he wouldn't clap at all.

No one remarked on it, there wasn't that rustle and stare that people do in groups to register disapproval or dismay. I didn't like the sound or the man's tense posture and repetitive movements. I was a kid, I assumed something was wrong with him. Then I became used to him. He was the man who clapped in church. Maybe, I thought, that's his way of praying, moving his body back and forth like he was bowing as he rapidly clapped his hands together. He was part of our community, and we all got used to him, and accepted him.

Many of us have had that experience – someone in a group or family who was odd or challenging or difficult or just irritating. But they were still welcome, still accepted.

That's the kind of approach I want to take with my inner community.

Because I'm a visual thinker, I have assigned the members of my inner community physical attributes. There's the Worst-Case Scenario one, who is constantly screaming about imminent peril. I picture that one as a soldier with a sword. She yells really loud. I'll tell her that I hear her, I appreciate her vigilance, but it's not actually dangerous right now. Sometimes there's a method to their messages. The Worst-Case Scenario screamer thinks she is protecting me by warning me all the time.

Then there's Barbara. My friend Juliette told me this one, and it's become an ongoing reference between us and our friends now. Barbara is any voice that is negative or destructive or cruel. When that voice chimes in we say "thanks for sharing, Barbara. It's time to sit down now and give someone else a chance to talk," or just "thanks for sharing, Barbara."

I have no idea why the name we use is Barbara, but there are quite a few of us now who know about Barbara. I've told clients about Barbara, and friends. No one has ever asked me to explain what the negative voices in our head are. Everyone, especially women, understands that part immediately. What's helpful is the separation of the message from the perception. Instead of believing I'm terrible, or stupid, or worthless, that those messages are fact or accurate or true, instead of fighting them or engaging with them, I imagine a person named Barbara saying them. That way, when I tell Barbara to be still, I've just popped that voice into another category. If that's something Barbara is saying, she could be wrong. There could be other voices who might challenge that. Barbara is not me.

Since so much of discernment is about listening deeply to ourselves, it can be helpful to understand who might be in our internal community talking trash. Who is not us, who is not telling the truth? Who might we need to have sit down and stop talking?

This is not an original idea, and many spiritual traditions and therapeutic modalities use a similar frame. This might not resonate for you, and that's fine, then this isn't for you. I'm happy for anyone who doesn't have a personal Greek chorus. If it does resonate, play with the idea for a while. Notice the messages that come up consistently for you. Does any image or characteristic emerge? I suggest to friends that if any voice talks to them in a way a friend never would, then it's not a valid voice. It's not true.

Your inner community may have positive as well as negative voices. It may also have an internalized version of people in your family, parents or grandparents. My paternal grandfather Ernest grew up poor in the Piedmont area in Italy. But he had lots of family pride. There is that member of my inner community that will, on occasion, remind me who is in my gene pool, and what is expected of us. That voice will say, with my grandfather's sometimes querulous, heavily accented English that I am a Peirolo, and should have the confidence of my ancestry.

Some believe that the Divine is in the inner community. For others it may be Ancestors or another manifestation of a spiritual energy. If your imagination doesn't connect with this exercise and no images or parts arise, you can borrow. Think about characters in fiction or film that connect with the noise that comes up in your head. Vampires or superheroes, talking bears or alien life forms, angels or devils. Who is in there? How can you make peace with the ones who aren't helpful and get them to stop talking or yelling or shrieking or whatever else they might be doing?

As you sit with this, consider if any voices or parts have come to the forefront. Are there supportive voices who carried you this far? Or are there negative voices who tell you that you're a failure and there is no point in thinking about your question, this whole idea of discernment is stupid anyway. Can you get curious about the negative voices? What might they being trying to protect or prevent?

A friend of mine once told me that she will put an empty chair in front of her and actually speak to parts as if they were there, in front of her, sitting in that chair, listening. I tried it and found it to be surprisingly moving.

As you continue through this process, try to stay aware of the noise, the static, that can come from this internal community. If it gets in the way of your discernment, if it clouds your ability to understand what information is surfacing, you may want to revisit this chapter and try any of the techniques listed here. Or make up your own.

If you find members of your inner community who are helpful, supportive, encouraging or grounding, what ways can you continue to access that? Is there a symbolic reminder of that energy you can have around you, like a small figure representing a supportive member of your inner community that you could place on your desk or bedside table?

Invitation to Explore

- Who is in your inner community? What do they wear or carry? Are they human, animal, alien, otherworldly? If you'd like to do creative work around the members of your inner community, try writing or drawing, or using any creative method to explore this.

- Is there a child, or you as a younger person? Who is it that encourages you to play? Who loves pets or Star Wars or hiking or something precious to you?

- Who are the positive and supportive voices?

- Who are the negative or unkind parts of your inner community?

- Is the Divine there, or your ancestors or any higher energy?

- Is there anyone from your family?

- How do these different parts interact with each other? If they are, indeed, a community, how are the good ones compassionate with the unskilled ones? Are there parts that protect you? Are the old protections still needed?

- Are there monsters? What do they say? Are you afraid of them? Is there anyone in the inner community who can help them?

- Did anything about this pertain to the question you are discerning? Are there any members of your inner community who can help you? Any you need to watch out for, who might be unreliable narrators?

Meditation with your senses

Imagine a room that is your mind, your awareness, the place where your inner community gathers. Put yourself in your imagination in that room or space. Look around. What do you see? Put your hands out, take a few steps. What does the floor feel like, or any wall space if it is there? Is it warm or cold? Do you smell anything?

Now imagine that the room is filling up with your inner community. How do they sound coming into the room? Where do they sit, what kind of gathering do they make? What do they carry? Are there any individuals who catch your attention? Do you want to interact with them? What does that bring up for you emotionally? What do you feel like in your stomach or chest, or shoulders, or wherever your body registers emotion? Are there any other members of your inner community you want to engage with? What is that like? What does that bring up for you? Does this group cooperate? Or do they fight with each other?

When you are done, sit quietly for a moment and survey your body, your mind, your spirit. What came up for you?

Your Thoughts

Part Three

The Stories that Support and Hinder

CHAPTER TWELVE

Children's Stories

I've always wanted to be a writer. I studied English and Creative Writing in college. I wrote short stories for my writing seminars, but I really wanted to write novels. Soon after graduation I was talking with my mother about my future. I was working as a waitress, but the plan was to use the time outside of work to focus on my writing, to finish the novel I had begun my senior year in college. It was a relief to be done with college. I felt like I finally had the time I needed and wanted to write the novel I never had time for when I was in school.

I was in the small, narrow kitchen of my apartment in Washington DC. We had phones that were still attached to the wall then and I couldn't move too far out of the kitchen, so I looked into the fridge.

"I always thought you'd write lovely children's books," my mother said.

I stood up, closed the fridge, and leaned against it, staring out the window.

She said it warmly, it was clearly one of those stories she told herself and her friends.

I had just graduated from Stanford, working my ass off to learn about literature and how to write. I finished my degree even though my father died the summer before my junior year. And it was the writing that drove me, this hunger to read, write, use my voice.

Children's books can be lovely and transformative, and I enjoy them. But I never wanted to write them. I never read them until I had children of my own. Women write children's books. That was my mother's narrative. Having a daughter who wrote small books for small children was a story my mother could get behind.

I don't remember what I said to my mother when she made that comment. I wouldn't have confronted her. She spent her whole life erecting elaborate constructions of narrative, much of it complete fantasy, and questioning it was ineffective and incendiary. But I mentally rejected her story with anger that still echoes across the intervening decades.

And yet. I can still feel her story, like broken glass on a bedroom floor; hard to avoid barefoot in the dark. I write things and then don't submit them. One rejection letter paralyses me and I stop submitting anything. It's as if my psyche has made an accommodation with the narrative box my mother put me in that day; you can write, but you can't publish, you can't be recognized as a writer of anything other than children's stories. Which I don't write.

We humans are meaning making machines. We make meaning by telling stories. We see stories the way we see faces; our eyes are primed to see patterns as facial features like the man in the moon, and our minds and spirits are primed for narrative. Stories can support us or limit us. A story can be useful at one point in our lives and then lose utility later. The stories we are told as children by our families, our culture, our religions, can echo through the rest of our lives. Stories are not the problem. The problem is believing that a story is real when it's not, accepting a false narrative as immutable fact rather than the fiction it is.

Children learn the difference between pretend and real when they are quite young. My young granddaughter Ruby often asks me if something is real or pretend. Or she'll tell me a story about the monster outside and then carefully label it "just pretend" which she says as one word "justpretend." But she's still relieved when I tell her that monsters aren't allowed at Nana's house, even pretend ones. I tell her the (justpretend) monsters are scared of me so they don't come near my house. She understands monsters are pretend, but she's still comforted by the idea that they are scared of me and stay away. I think of that with the stories in my head. Even the justpretend ones can still scare me if I'm not careful.

Inordinate attachment

"Spiritual exercises which have as their purpose the conquest of self and the regulation of one's life in such a way that no decision is made under the influence of any inordinate attachment." (SE # 21) Ignatius wrote that. There's plenty packed into that sentence, but what intrigues me is the inordinate attachment I have to certain narratives. The inordinate attachment we as a culture have to specific stories. Learning how to make decisions without the influence of our inordinate attachment to limiting or damaging narratives is the point of this section.

Alcoholism and drug addiction are easy to understand as inordinate attachments. My attachment to alcohol was inordinate, extraordinary. A friend once asked me about my sobriety, saying, "don't you miss the taste of good wine?"

I laughed. Taste, conviviality, ease, all those things that are associated with an appreciation of wine or spirits were lost to me for most of the last years of my drinking. I enjoyed expensive single malt scotch, I savored the peaty aroma, but I would have consumed whatever was put in front of me to achieve the impact of alcohol; the snick of release when the hypervigilant part of my brain shut off. No matter that release was often accompanied by blackouts where I lost hours. I was attached to the impact of alcohol, any alcohol, not the taste or vintage.

Towards the end of my drinking, when I knew I was an alcoholic but wasn't ready to stop, I went back to my apartment in Washington DC one day and I didn't recognize it. I wasn't drunk at that moment. It was the middle of the afternoon, and I looked around and felt like I was not actually in my home. I knew the furniture was mine. I understood intellectually that I was standing in the correct apartment at the correct address. But on a fundamental level I didn't recognize it because I couldn't determine what was real any longer. My life, my mind, my body were acutely dysregulated.

A few months earlier I had that same experience with my face in the mirror. That time I was drunk. I was in a bar in Adams Morgan and went to the ladies' room and saw my face in the mirror and I didn't know who I was. Literally, not figuratively, I was so drunk I didn't recognize my own face. I knew it had to be me because there wasn't anyone else in the bathroom. Did Hemingway write about this, I thought to myself, looking at the young woman with long dark hair and brown eyes like my grandmother's?

I thought I was losing my mind. The narrative in my head was that I had to hide this from anyone around me or they'd take me to a sinister mental hospital and make me have a lobotomy. This was in the eighties; people weren't handing out lobotomies. But that didn't matter, since I was now only tenuously connected to reality and I had seen that movie about Frances Farmer, an actress in the nineteen thirties who was lobotomized.

When, a few years later, I realized I was an alcoholic, I was completely relieved. I wasn't crazy, I was a drunk! Oddly, that was a story I celebrated. For many, it's a shameful admission, for me it was the key to get out of the trap of the narrative that I was insane. I told my friends I was an alcoholic with joyful exultation. They weren't surprised at the alcoholic part; they had seen the trouble I could get into when drunk. They just didn't expect me to be so happy about the admission.

I've had friends who responded to a diagnosis of ADHD in much the same way; the relief of having an explanation for patterns of behavior that didn't make sense without that narrative. These stories can be supportive, bringing order out of chaos. For some, identifying with others with the same diagnosis can connect them with a community of support. For others, it can begin to heal shame and the sense there was something wrong with them. For me, I stopped being worried that I'd be institutionalized. I just had to figure out a way to not drink alcohol anymore.

It took me much longer to understand that I could be inordinately attached to behaviors that were not identified by society as deleterious to health. I've struggled to maintain a sane and balanced approach to work. The fact that I am writing this while we are on vacation, looking out at the sun dancing on Puget Sound, might indicate that I still have growth opportunities around the whole work life balance thing.

In the past few years, I've come to understand that we can be inordinately attached to ideas and narratives. Think of someone who you disagree with on social or political issues. Don't they sometimes seem inordinately attached to their viewpoint as the only correct interpretation of events or history? Do they stay adamant even in the face of facts and figures that refute their cherished notions? When we ask "how can someone believe that in spite of . . ." we are noting another's inordinate attachment to a specific narrative. But don't most of us do the same thing? When I sit across the table from one of my cousins who has very different political beliefs than I do, isn't she wondering how I can vote the way I do knowing what she knows? She tries to reframe my narrative, as I am trying to reframe hers.

We don't always question the stories we are told, and their validity over time. A key piece of our discernment process is making the stories we were told visible as stories; constructs rather than actual reality. Then we can decide if they are still real and valid for us, or if they are just pretend, outmoded or even harmful. And we can see if we are inordinately attached to any of our narratives in a way that causes us to become enmeshed in a world view that no longer serves us.

Many of the stories are cultural. In our patriarchal, capitalist system, which was built on white supremacy, damaging narratives are perpetuated about who gets to have power and wealth and what role work should play in our lives. Some of the stories are familial. Families have stories that support and/or limit. Stories from our religious traditions, even a religion we have left behind, can trail behind us loudly, like cans tied to a car bumper that rattle behind us.

The Spiritual Exercises are grounded in Biblical stories about Jesus. The Big Book has an entire section devoted to stories about different people from a variety of backgrounds and their experience with alcoholism and sobriety. The stories are updated occasionally to more accurately reflect the culture in which we live. Story is central to most spiritual teachings.

But these stories are accepted by Ignatius and Wilson as true. Their spiritual paths are less interested in investigating which stories might not be true, which narratives are misleading us. The themes are there. When Ignatius warns us against the blandishments of the Devil, I hear that as being critical of false narratives. Discernment of spirits is, to me, examining the veracity of the stories we are told.

When Wilson talks about a moral inventory in the Fourth Step, he describes it as ". . . personal inventory. *This was Step Four.* A business which takes no regular inventory usually goes broke. Taking a commercial inventory is a fact-finding and fact-facing process. It is an effort to discover the truth about the stock-in-trade. One object is to disclose damaged or unsaleable goods, to get rid of them promptly and without regret. If the owner of the business is to be successful, he cannot fool himself about values." (BB p. 64) Wilson focuses on the "flaws in our make-up which caused our failure." (BB p. 64). I prefer to focus on the stories we've been told about who we get to be, and to decide which we want to keep and which we want to "get rid of promptly and without regret."

I first heard the invitation to "reframe the narrative" when I was in graduate school, from the woman who is now my spiritual director. The invitation is grounded in feminism and social justice work. Cultural narratives are perpetuated by those who are culturally dominant. They attempt to keep those who are marginalized from gaining power or agency. Testing those narratives is a subversive act, one that has been critical to my growth. I've said "reframe the narrative" so often to co-workers, clients and friends that it's become something of a catch phrase, they tease me about it, but it is important.

Certain narrative themes come up for me and the people I know, and those are what I am including in this section. Generally, the themes I hear most often are about money and financial security; power and who gets to have it; home, children, family and who takes care of them; rest and when and how you get to take care of yourself; the role spirituality or moral values should play in your life; who gets to be heard and centered and who is silenced or ignored; our relationship with time and the seasons of our life. But you may have very different themes. Explore what you come up with even if it's not on this list.

As you look through the following stories, consider writing any key narratives that emerge for you, doing an inventory if you will. Which of the stories that you carry are supportive, and which are limiting? Are there stories that have aspects of both? I suggest capturing your key learnings from this section in the space you are using to track your discernment. It's ok if you don't see how they fit yet. But as you review the stories, see how any of your discoveries impact the work you've done so far. See if and how any on-going narratives may be impacting your decisions by continuing to journal and sit with what comes up for you.

Your Thoughts

CHAPTER THIRTEEN

Work History

What do we believe about work? Let's think about a kind of work history that isn't the history of the jobs you've had or the work you've done, but the history of your unique understanding of what work is and the role of work in a person's life. What are the stories you tell yourself about work – work in general, or your career or a specific industry?

Stories about work can change, depending on the season of your life and your perspective. When I was a teenager, one night after dinner, my father was talking to my sister and me about careers – a common occurrence. My mother stopped him and asked him, about us, "What if they get married? What if they want to have children?"

My father stopped talking. He was silent for a moment. It was clear he had never considered this. It was a revelation to all of us that my father, for all his planning and direction for our future, had never considered that one or both of his daughters might want to marry or be a mother. We were in high school. It was the end of the 70s. Neither one of my grandmothers worked outside the home, and they had four and five children, respectively. Both my grandmothers had their first child in their twenties and their last children in their forties. My mother hadn't worked outside of the home for years. But my father disregarded an entire cultural narrative when it came to his plans for his daughters. That was, at first, a powerfully supportive story for me, that gender roles are fungible, a product of a cultural imagination that could be unimagined if you had the intellect, desire and conviction to reframe them.

However, when I did have children, I felt like I had failed my father. He was dead by then, so I couldn't reframe the narrative by talking to him. But I remember being home with my newborn son, feeling like I had wasted my college education because I had a child soon after graduation and didn't go to work immediately at a big corporation. That was not a helpful narrative, or one that was especially useful or accurate.

When I did get to corporate America, I was a few years behind my peers because I stayed home until my youngest was three. I felt vaguely embarrassed that I had kids in my twenties, when my colleagues didn't have children until their thirties or forties.

Decades later, those same people who had children after I did complained about going through menopause while their kids were going through puberty, or paying for college a few years shy of retirement.

Many decisions carry gifts and burdens, especially decisions about family. The point is that my narratives about being a working mother have continued to evolve throughout my life.

Who taught you about work?

Think about your childhood. Who taught you about work? What lessons did you take in from your family and culture? Who was permitted to work and who was not? Whose work was valued and whose was not? Was work something that adults seemed to enjoy, or was it oppressive or dangerous? Were the adults proud of their work?

Most of my understanding of work came from my father. He dressed up in a suit and tie and went to work in an office. He travelled often. I knew where he worked and what skills he used since he taught them to me, but I didn't really understand what he did.

But I learned about who was allowed to work from my mother. My mother was a very intelligent woman who was going to pursue a graduate degree in oceanography when she met my father. This was in the late 1950s. She said she turned down the graduate program to get married. She told this story often; it was important that we knew that she was smart enough to go to graduate school. She never explained why she thought that getting married meant she couldn't go to grad school, because she did not seem to believe she had any other option. Which is an example of how narratives form our understanding of our place in the world. The only women on my mother's side of the family who worked outside the home were divorced or widowed.

When my father started graduate school, my parents moved from the Seattle area to the East Coast, shortly after I was born. I can't imagine getting into a car with all your possessions and driving cross country less than a week after giving birth to your first child. But that's what they did. I was born in August, and his classes were starting. A man's graduate degree and career was worth any amount of uprooting, even if it meant his wife traveling across the country sitting on a round cushion because she was still healing from an episiotomy.

When we lived in Seattle in the mid-seventies, my mother was admitted to the University of Washington law school. I remember her studying for the LSAT, and how she seemed different to me, happier, engaged. I was in middle school, and the thought of my mother going to law school seemed cool. Then my father was transferred to Los Angeles for work, so we moved, and she never went to law school.

She stopped working after that and poured her energies into real estate. She fixed up the houses we lived in, then she tried to make a profit from the sale when we moved the next time. She said if you baked bread before an open house, the house would sell more quickly. She bought ready-made heat and serve loaves and kept them in the oven until the house was fragrant and the bread cooked to a hard stick that would be thrown away when everyone was gone. From what I remember, she made money for the family that way. I know that our houses kept getting bigger and bigger, as my parents tried to reinvest to not have to pay taxes on their capital gains.

The narrative in my family was that my father had the career. My mother's work, in or out of the house, was never considered work. No one ever made a comment on the fact that she was the one who turned down opportunities for education and career if they conflicted with her husband's job. No one considered the work entailed in raising children, buying and selling houses, stripping wallpaper and repainting rooms and moving every couple of years.

What kind of work is important?

My father's father, Ernest, was a cabinetmaker. My mother didn't get along with my father's family, but to everyone's surprise, my grandfather found a wooden bed somewhere and fixed it up for my mother. I think it was a peace offering, a desire to stay connected to his oldest son's family. The bed had a dark wooden frame, with curved wood and elaborate carvings on the top of the headboard that you could remove for a simpler look.

My mother didn't like the bed. I slept in it for most of the time I was growing up. I would stand up and take the carvings off the top of the headboard and look at them. My grandfather had carved them to replace the originals that were missing or damaged. I was fascinated by what he could make the wood do. Whorls and tendrils in an arch with wooden pegs that slipped easily in and out of the top of the headboard. He told me that the original frame of the bed was made from wood that was heated and then bent, so it curved in majestic, rounded flourishes with no corners, only smooth curves. He touched wood like he appreciated it, savored it. I remember all his tools hung neatly on pegboards in the garage that he used as a workshop. He wasn't a warm man, and we didn't see my grandparents often because of the conflict with my mother, but I remember how he talked about his work. He said that his brother Anselmo, who was still in Italy, was the real artist, a woodcarver, an artisan. The way my grandfather talked about art taught me that artists were important. He would listen to opera and cry. He spoke English, French and Italian. As a young person, he read *Les Misérables* in French late into the night, even though he had to get up early to work. He never said what kind of work he did as a teenager, although I believe it was agricultural, but he told me what he read. Writers, artist, and craftspeople were important, valuable, gifted.

When work is bad: Neural Smudging

Bad or abusive jobs can impact our understanding of ourselves, our competence and skills, for years. We have an understanding of who we are at work. Often our understandings are inaccurate because of the system or culture in which we work.

There's a corollary in our body that's called neural smudging. We all carry a mental image of our bodies. It's called proprioception. It lets us know where we are in space. You can close your eyes and touch your index fingers together tip to tip because you know where your hands are even when you can't see them. That's proprioception.

When you have chronic pain, it can mess with your proprioception. This is how "phantom limb" pain happens, pain that a person senses in a limb that has been amputated. Essentially, your body's map of itself in space gets it wrong.

I've had chronic pain in my hips for about fifteen years. Two surgeries helped, but didn't erase the pain. I've been to excellent physical therapists over the years, and the one I'm seeing now told me that my proprioception is off. I can't "see" my hips in a mental model.

Try this. Do a body scan right now. Close your eyes. Start at the top of your head and sweep down through your shoulder, hips, knees and feet. Easy, right? When I do that, I can't imagine my hips. I see head, shoulders, trunk, legs, feet. No hips. Blank space. This is called "neural smudging." I like that phrase, as if my brain had blurred the lines around the source of my chronic pain, like an artist will do with charcoal on a white page.

The problem with neural smudging is that since I don't "see" my hips anymore, I don't use them to do what they are supposed to do – move my legs. Instead, I use my lower back. Which hurts my lower back. When I swim I should be using my glutes to kick, not my lower back. But my proprioception has erased my glutes, so I use my lower back. Which aches when I get out of the pool.

The solution is to redraw that missing part of my body in my brain's map. In addition to a bunch of exercises where I isolate my hips, the PT told me to tell myself that I have glutes. Literally say "I have glutes, I have glutes" as I swim. I tried this with internal eye roll when I was doing laps, but to my surprise it worked.

When I got my head around the fact that chronic pain could re-map my understanding of how my body takes up space in the world, I began to wonder what chronically painful work environments do to us. What gets erased, smudged? What becomes inaccessible? What is overworked instead?

Many of us have experiences of chronic difficulties at work. I would argue that we also have a work proprioception, a sense of who we are and who we get to be at our jobs. And that chronic stress or discrimination can cause the same neural smudging or distortion that chronic physical pain does.

What does that mean at work? For me I've noticed that I don't accurately assess my skills in the workplace. It's like I'm wearing glasses that distort and erase my abilities. This makes me over prepare, since I worry about skills I have. A good example of this is public speaking. I do it often, I have a podcast, and I even teach other people how to present more effectively. But I don't see that I have skills there. When I need to present, I will over prepare, and rehearse way more than needed. It takes up a lot of time and energy that could be spent elsewhere.

I also don't always perceive damage quickly. Since I'm inured to a certain level of pain at work, I don't always perceive a slight or aggressive behavior in the moment, when I could address it most effectively. It's not until much later, if at all, that I'll see it. Sometimes, I won't even understand what's happening until I recount an episode to a friend who will say, "wait, what? He said what?!?"

I've never had a job where I've felt a sense of psychological safety. I've felt it in other areas of my life, and I know that with that sense of safety I am more creative, effective and happy. In corporate work settings I have usually been clenched, braced for an impact that may or may not arrive. Being hypervigilant takes up so much energy. Energy that could be flowing to more constructive areas like creativity, problem solving, interpersonal relationships.

When it comes to my physical well-being, I understand now that living with chronic pain for years before addressing it rewired my brain. My perception of pain, which areas of my body I could use effectively and not, indeed even something as fundamental as how I walk is still impacted by all that pain, day in and day out. I have PT exercises and ways to understand the pain that is helping me heal and reconnect with a more accurate understanding of my body and how it moves through space.

But what about the chronic pain of living with microaggressions, discrimination, hypervigilance and fear at work? How many of us have experienced work neural smudging in our inability to understand our skills and competencies; a problem seeing injuries as injuries; the discomfort of overcorrecting or overextending certain skills like over preparing to compensate for not seeing that we're better than we give ourselves credit for?

And what are the exercises that we can use to heal? I've largely left the corporate world, and only come in as a visitor to help others. What do we do for the people who are still in the thick of that chronic pain?

As you consider your work history, especially if you are in a group that is marginalized, underrepresented and/or discriminated against, ask yourself if your perceptions of yourself are accurate or if you, too, could have been misled by the neural smudging of too much work pain for too long.

Work Timeline

One exercise that might be useful here for people who are older is to do a work timeline. Write a long line and start at one end with your first job. Mine was delivering the Washington Post to my neighbors. I had to get up very early. I was thirteen or fourteen. I remember how cold it was in the winter. I remember delivering the paper on Christmas morning at 5am and looking through a window and seeing a sleepy father walking down the stairs behind two excited little children who were tearing through the house to the Christmas tree and presents.

What are the jobs you had and what did you learn from them?

What jobs represented inflection points? Your first job as an ICU nurse, or your first job after you left the military.

If you have work that is your true work as well as work that is econ, put multiple lines on your work history. We can decide what we consider to be work, and I invite us all to open the aperture to include caring for children or sick family members, our art, participation in a church or any other community engagement or social action.

Invitation to Explore

- Who did you learn about work from? What did they teach you?

- Was there work or labor that was celebrated in your family? Work that was discounted or slighted? Why?

- What narratives did your family have about work and community or society? For example, was your family involved in a union or were they part of a family business?

- Did your family want you to pursue a particular career or type of employment? Did you? What was the reaction if you did or did not? Do you have other siblings or family members who made a different choice than you did about doing what your family wanted? What was their experience?

- Did your family have stories about what kind of profession or work was important or valuable? Doctor, lawyer, engineer, welder, priest; families often have a hierarchy of which professions "matter."

- Consider your work timeline, including both true work and econ where applicable. What patterns do you see? Are there any surprises?

- What about your work history is joyful or rewarding?

- What is hard, hurtful or sad to recall?

- What narratives surface for you that might not be helpful or supportive?

- Have you experienced any work neural smudging?

- Are there any implications from this exploration for your discernment question? If there are, write them down and capture them in whatever space you are using for this process.

Your Thoughts

CHAPTER FOURTEEN

Money

I went to Stanford University in the 80s. There were plenty of rich kids, sons and daughters of movie stars and politicians. Lots of famous last names, the kind where you say, "*oh that (*insert famous name here)." Once I walked into the wrong room at a party when I was trying to find a bathroom and there was a pile of cocaine on a table that was inches high. At first, I thought someone had dumped a five-pound bag of flour on the table because it never occurred to me that anyone would have that much cocaine in one place in real life – it was something you only saw in movies. I remember a woman standing next to the table turning to look at me with that calculating eye, wondering if I was the kind of person she would invite in. Evidently not. I quickly left the room and closed the door.

I went to a dinner party my junior year, a few months after my father died. Before he died he was too sick to work, so money was tight. I worked in the coffee shop on campus and rode a bicycle since I had no car, and I didn't fly home very often. I rarely bought clothes, or food that wasn't included in my meal plan.

The woman to my left at the dinner party was talking loudly about a trip to Europe and she turned to me, tilting her face so the host, who she had a crush on, could see her – *look at me talking to your odd quiet friend,* – and she asked where I had traveled. What was my favorite spot in Europe?

"I've never been to Europe," I said. I thought to myself, bitch, please, I own two pairs of trousers and I don't have enough money to buy a beer right now, so how the hell am I supposed to get to Europe?

"Why not?" she said. I looked at her. She was genuinely curious. And I realized that this young woman, who was probably, like me, 19 or 20, had never met someone who couldn't afford to travel to Europe. It was literally outside of her realm of understanding. I felt a searing humiliation, and a rage, and a sense of being out of place that was so acute I felt ill.

This was where my resentment towards people with money started. Don't get me wrong, there have been times when I have had money. And I've also been so broke I wasn't sure how I was going to feed my children. A lack of money and financial security has caused me great difficulties. So, when I come across people who are like that woman at the dinner party, people who have no comprehension that most of the world lives without the kind of privilege and ease they do, I get peevish. While also understanding that I have privilege and ease that others do not.

Most of us don't see real money, actual coins or currency, that often anymore. It's usually numbers on a screen; a device or card used to transfer pieces of code from one imagined space in the ether to another. For something that isn't quite real, money takes up lots of emotional and mental space for most of us. How we think about money, especially if we have been impacted by financial trauma, food insecurity or lack of access to secure housing, can be one of the heaviest narratives to sort through in a discernment process about work.

Money was fraught when I was growing up. My mother liked nice things. And we had many nice things, fancy cars, big houses, nice clothes, comfortable vacations to warmer climes. But my parents couldn't seem to manage their finances. I remember them sitting down to "do the bills" once a month and getting into huge fights. They would spread paper bills and a checkbook across the round wooden kitchen table and end up getting in massive arguments. Money was something that made my mother yell. Whenever the word "bills" came up, I would get nervous, like watching storm clouds gather. My parents would spread the bills across the table and wait until we went to bed, but I knew how it would end, the fights. My mother screaming, my father's low murmur in response.

My mother used to "borrow" my sister's babysitting money. I didn't like babysitting, but my sister did lots of it as a teenager and made good money, which she kept in cash in her bedroom. We were living in a big house with a fancy car in the driveway and my mother would borrow twenty dollars from my sister to buy milk and cigarettes, or thirty dollars for something else. I don't know if she ever returned that money, but I never saw that she did. My mother would encourage me to babysit since my sister had more work than she could handle. But it seemed stupid to me to do something I didn't like – babysitting – to make money that someone else would take from me.

After my divorce, when the kids were young, money was very tight. I kept moving farther out of town where rent was cheaper. I split my own firewood, swinging the heavy axe, because the wood stove was cheaper than the electric base boards. One day we came home, and the little A frame had a big notice on the front door that if I didn't pay my electric bill the electricity would be shut off. I pulled it down before the kids, who were just learning how to read, could understand what it said. What it meant.

I didn't realize until much later in life that those things were financial trauma, which impacted how I think about money. I didn't know what financial trauma was. No one taught me about money. No one taught me about saving or how to balance a checkbook, or that you shouldn't use credit cards unless you could pay them off at the end of every month. My family had money but couldn't manage it. I didn't have money for many years. As a result, I didn't teach my children about money when they were growing up.

Fear of financial insecurity is such a struggle for me that I gave it a nickname – FOFI. A friend says it sounds like a fluffy children's cartoon character. In my imagination it is a monster. I have realized that FOFI isn't connected to how much money I actually have. I have been calm with very little in the bank, and nervous with an amount I might once have considered to be a fortune. FOFI can obscure any accurate assessment of my real financial situation or the actual financial implications of a decision. Looking without judgement at the lens of fear that I wear has helped me to understand this is an area where I need help. I have a financial adviser who I listen to, and I pay a CPA and bookkeeper to help me with my business finances. I call my trusted Aunt Tanya when I have any financial decision to make so I can get an unbiased view that's focused on reality and not distorted by the fear goggles I tend to wear.

For me, financial trauma and fear of financial insecurity show up in different ways. For years after my divorce, I just wouldn't open the mail. All the bills would pile up and I would ignore them until the envelopes arrived with the big red lettering about collections. I was too afraid to open my mail, even when I had money to pay most of my bills.

I wouldn't spend money on needed items like a new appliance or home repair because spending all at once scared me. At other times, I would overspend. I bought a quilt I didn't need on a department store credit card because I wanted to be cozy, and I thought I deserved it. I couldn't pay off the credit card and it went into collections and followed me around on my credit report for seven years. I still have the quilt, because it's a nice quilt, but also because it reminds me of a time in my life when I did not spend in a way that was congruent with what I was earning.

I've spent much of my career in advertising, an entire industry built on getting people to spend money on things they don't necessarily need. I've watched smart, insightful strategic planners spend weeks figuring out how to get people to buy a particular type of butter.

I've also seen people who have achieved the big job and the fancy house and all the trappings that they wanted and yet rarely see their spouse or children, and have little time for anything other than work. I remember a woman I worked with years ago telling me that she and her husband both worked such demanding jobs that they rarely saw each other except in passing, when they handed over the care of their young children to the other one as he or she returned from the airport. She looked so sad as she told me this, so exhausted, standing in the office and realizing what her life had become. I didn't know her well, but I was afraid she was going to start crying. I could feel her desolation. Up until that moment I thought I wanted her life with the fancy job, the money, the husband, the financial security. We were selling advertising. We weren't saving lives or helping people, we were just feeding more fuel into the engine of want.

Understanding what stories you tell yourself about money and financial security can be important in your discernment process. I've known people in their late twenties with good jobs who refuse any career risk, or fight having the second child their wife wants, because they worry about not having enough money to retire three decades in the future. Others calmly take on six figure student loan debt in their thirties or forties to pursue an advanced degree, and believe it is an investment in their future.

For women

When I'm doing a negotiation training or talking about women and salaries, I often ask women to consider that their current state may not be their future state. Women who are married, especially women with young children, need to consider that they may not be married to that person by the time they get to retirement. Have your own money, I tell them. Have a career or skills that you can use even if you are coming back to the workplace after a break for having kids or staying home with them. Raising children is work, and should be valued as such. But the kids will grow up and leave home. What will you do then?

I also tell them something that I first heard from a venture capitalist in Seattle. I met this woman at an event a few years ago. We were both older, late forties for her and mid-fifties for me. She said that a woman's peak earning potential is over by the time she is in her mid-fifties, where professional men hit their peak in their late fifties and sixties. I hope things will change, but I tell women to try to make as much money as they can between forty and fifty because they don't know how much longer they will be valued in the workplace, or want to put up with the sexism and ageism.

Stories about money can also be supportive. I grew up on stories, perhaps apocryphal, of my mother's grandmother, Nonie. My grandmother Frances told me the stories of her mother, who she never got along well with, but who she clearly respected. After she became a young widow, Nonie went to San Francisco to meet with Ghirardelli, of chocolate fame, who had been a business associate of her husband's. She convinced him to invest in a business she started. She was quite successful, although she had a number of ups and downs. She never remarried and ran her businesses on her own.

At one point, the story goes, she owned a fruit drying plant in Medford, Oregon. My grandmother was young at the time, but she remembers hearing people running through the street one night yelling that there was a fire at the plant. Nonie and her four daughters raced over to the plant to see the buildings on fire, and the fire fighters standing idly by the trucks, smoking cigarettes. Men in white hoods rode horses in circles around the plant. Nonie was a woman, an immigrant, and a Catholic. That was enough to get the Ku Klux Klan to burn her business to the ground, and for the firefighters to stand around and watch. She left Medford, started over, and rebuilt her fortune again.

How much of my understanding of what I could accomplish as a single mother was shaped by stories about my great grandmother? Would it have been different if I'd heard stories about a woman who was broken by grief after her husband died and drank herself to death? Or one who sought the shelter and support of another man, another husband?

Women can have complicated relationships with money. Women are paid less than men, and women of color paid less than white women. After the divorce of an opposite sex couple, a woman will, generally speaking, be worse off financially while a man will be better off. Women still do the majority of housework as well as caregiving for children and aging parents. Which may mean less time to work or fewer opportunities for career advancement if the advancement is connected to the ability to work long hours, travel or move.

It can be hard to set boundaries around money, to believe we get to have our own finances or savings, regardless of our relationship status. I've seen women co-sign for cars or student loans for their partners or children and be saddled with crushing debt that isn't even theirs. I've known parents who have nothing saved for retirement but take out loans to pay for their child's college education. It's hard to say no to your children, or partners, especially when we already carry conflicted or unresolved issues about money.

Invitation to Explore

- What did you learn from your family about money?

- Were their fights over money? Was there gambling or reckless spending?

- Was there a lack of money? Were there cycles of doing well and then cycles of doing badly?

- Did anyone ever formally teach you about money? Did anyone show you how to write a check or open a bank account? Did they talk about or demonstrate saving money? Did you learn about budgeting or living within your means? What was the attitude towards debt?

- Did your family ever run out of money? What did "running out of money" mean? Did it mean that your family couldn't go on vacation or buy a new car, or did it mean that there wasn't enough food? Were you ever food insecure, or unhoused?

- Was someone in your family miserly, refusing to buy basic necessities like clothing, food or shoes even when there was enough money in the bank to do so? What impact did that have on you?

- Did people around you spend money on themselves? Who was allowed to do that? Was there a male relative who loved to shop for clothes? A female relative with expensive hobbies? Were they judged or celebrated?

- Was or is there someone you could call to get money in an emergency? If you had an unexpected dental emergency or car problem, could you get $1000 from a family member? $500? $100? If not, how does that impact you?

- What attitudes do you have about people with money? People who lack financial stability?

- Do you feel like you deserve financial security? Have you ever self-sabotaged your finances, spending recklessly rather than starting an emergency savings account?

- Do you generally have an attitude of abundance – "there is enough, things will work out for me" or scarcity – "there won't be enough, this will be taken from me, I have to compete for scarce resources"?

- Does anything that arises for you in this exploration impact the decision you are making? Even if you're not sure yet, it is good to capture key insights here to consider later.

Invitation for women

- What stories do you have about women and money? Did women in your family and community spend money on themselves, or did they do without, wearing ratty undergarments or broken-down shoes?

- When you grew up, did women have their own money? Did you have, as I did, the concept of 'mad money', twenty bucks tucked in your bra for a cab home?

- Where you saw divorce as you grew up, how did the women fare? How about the men? Did fathers stay involved and fulfill their financial obligations? What happened as the divorced people aged? Did they have enough money to retire? Who took care of them when they became ill?

- Did women in your family know about money? Were they good businesspeople, successful entrepreneurs or have vibrant long-lasting careers? Which women had financial security and why?

- What happened when a woman had her own money? Was she celebrated or considered to be selfish or arrogant?

- Did you see women help each other out in their careers and community, giving advice or sharing opportunities? Or did they guard what they had and try to undercut other women?

- Where did you see women who had good financial boundaries? Where did you see women who did not? How are your financial boundaries?

- How much do you know about money? Where your knowledge is missing, have you sought out information from reputable sources, or found a financial planner or advisor?

If money is troublesome for you as it is for me and many of us, try not to judge yourself. Just understand that you may also need additional perspectives to help you make decisions. Again, the goal here is to understand what stories impact your decision and which narratives you want to examine more closely and which you want to let go of altogether.

Your Thoughts

CHAPTER FIFTEEN

Quitting

Who gets to quit and how is that framed? When do you get to stop doing the thing you were doing and why?

Our culture celebrates perseverance. I remember once watching a sports channel that was celebrating the perseverance of endurance athletes. They showed a video of a women finishing a marathon. Her legs stopped holding her up, her entire body was shaking, and she crawled across the finish line, at the end writhing on her stomach like a worm. According to the commentator, we were supposed to admire this behavior. I just thought it was stupid. Why would you push your body to such extremes it stopped functioning? It seemed like she was perpetuating a kind of violence against herself, and I felt the same way I would have if I was watching someone intentionally slam their fingers in a car door over and over again.

Quitting is hard. I have tended to stay too long in bad jobs and bad relationships. Many of us do. We hope it will get better, we look on the bright side, we worry about being alone or not getting another job. We think of all the time or money we invested; we worry about what other people will think of us. Sometimes there are spiritual, cultural or religious reasons for us to continue on a particular course.

If the question you are discerning has to do with you stopping doing something you have been doing, then it may help you to look at any stories you carry about quitting. Often when we think of quitting, we are hearing someone else's narrative in our heads. Which can make it difficult to ascertain what our interior wisdom is inviting us to consider.

I was talking with a young friend who was trying to make a decision about what kind of law to pursue soon after he passed the Bar. None of the available job opportunities interested him. I asked if he was interested in something besides law.

"But then I'll have wasted the last three years of my life," he said, insisting that he couldn't consider any option that didn't include practicing law. I realized, talking to him, how many men are still told they need to be the breadwinner, the provider, especially if they want to have children. And there is a consistent cultural message that time is short and should not be wasted.

What is waste? How many people end up in a career based on decisions they made when they were in their late teens or early twenties? What happens if you outgrow those early decisions as you mature? Education, formal or otherwise, is never wasted. We can build on it over time. Sometimes we only see in hindsight that our experiences may hold together thematically. Non-traditional experience can also teach us skills. I know that being a single mom made me focused and organized.

Once I was hiring for an entry level position at a tech start-up. One candidate held a fancy internship in the summer breaks from his elite college education. Another had put himself through a state school by refinishing bathtubs. He told me about refinishing bathtubs in our job interview. It was clear he had to work long hours doing tough physical labor and still excelled in school. I hired him for that reason, and he was a great hire. I've known executives who won't hire someone if they haven't ever waited tables, because they believe experience in the service industry is key to success at businesses that rely on client relationships. I've given my business card to teenagers selling mobile phone plans at the mall because they were clearly such natural salespeople I wanted to hire them when they finished school. These people stopped doing one type of job but carried skills and attitudes they had learned into the next job.

Understand your narratives about leaving one thing to do another and see if they support you or hinder you. Start by examining the language you use. Is it quitting by quitters or is it sailing into a new adventure? Is it embracing change and growing or is it wasting time, education or opportunity? Is failure part of your narrative about changing course?

Having grown up Catholic, I felt like a failure when I divorced in my twenties and became a single mom. It was a visceral experience, as if everyone could see that I was a failure because I had two little kids and no wedding ring. "Quitting" that marriage, even though it wasn't my choice, was loaded with emotional and cultural baggage for me. Then, to my surprise, I felt a strong sense of relief. Since I'd already "failed" according to the social and cultural narratives in my head, I was now free to live a life that was of my own design, rather than one that conformed to what my family and culture said I should do. The relief was visceral as well, a lightness as if I had taken off a restrictive corset of expectations and could now comfortably fill my lungs with air.

Invitation to explore

- What stories do you have around changing course?

- Are the stories gendered? Was there a different experience for men and women?

- Do you have examples of people in your family who quit, who left a marriage or changed jobs or dropped out of college or graduate school? What stories were you told about them?

- Were there people who hung in until the bitter end? They stayed at a job they hated, or in a marriage that stifled them, or in a religion that told them they were sinful and bad. What were you told about them and their choices?

- Were there any people in your community who quit a lucrative career to pursue a passion that paid less? Was that celebrated or condemned? Were they accused of wasting their career standing and experience or expensive education or congratulated for finding something they loved to do?

- Do you think you have permission to quit? To leave, to change directions and say goodbye to old ways of working or being in relationship? Who does have that permission?

- Are people allowed to grow out of something? Are they able to incorporate a new way of understanding who they are? This could be a man realizing he's bisexual or a woman deciding to leave corporate law and become an organic farmer.

- Who does get to change direction as they mature and leave things behind?

- Are there implications for your discernment process from what you're considering in this section?

Meditation with your senses

If you are discerning a question that involves an ending that others might frame as "quitting" a meditation might be helpful. Whether you are leaving a career, a relationship, or graduate school, imagine your life if you left the thing you are considering leaving.

Imagine yourself in the new life. Picture where you live in that new life, what your day is like from the time you wake up in the morning. Imagine with your senses; touch, sound, smell, sight, taste. Spend time imagining being in this new life. See what comes up for you. What does it feel like? What emotions arise? Do you have anxiety? Grief? Relief? Excitement? Fear? Don't judge anything that comes up for you, just note it.

Your Thoughts

CHAPTER SIXTEEN

Power

I worked for a start-up in the early nineties. We had a cool new technology, and I was part of a group that was selling it to media companies. I had been working on a big deal for a long time, and had developed a good working relationship with the client.

I was in New York for a meeting. The client was out of town, so he joined via video. I sat in a fancy conference room in a chair that probably cost as much as my car. There were about eight men around the table, most of them from Dublin, with fetching accents. I was the only woman in the room. The men disregarded me, I think they thought I was the secretary. About halfway through the discussion of whatever we were hashing out, the client had to leave.

"Stephanie can finish the meeting," he said. The screen went dark. The men turned to me with a new respect, now that I was virtually deputized. I felt it, the rush of power, the social capital of that baton pass. It felt like a drug, a sudden saturation of vindication – these men who had, like so many others, disregarded and dismissed me, now needed me to get them the money they wanted for the deals they wanted to do.

Who has power? How do they get it? How do they keep it? How do they use it? Most of us carry narratives around power. In my thirties, when that meeting took place, I was deeply captivated by the narrative that money and prestige in the capitalist system were the way to accrue power. I thought power would protect me and my children. Enough money meant I could buy a house, and not be at the mercy of a landlord. I could pay for better schools, save for my kids to go to college. I thought if I got enough power the men I worked with would stop harassing me, discounting me, undercutting me. I knew what was happening to me was gendered, but I thought that if I had enough power, if I was running a company or a division then that would protect me. I worked long hours doing stressful, difficult work and travelled extensively. I didn't realize how deeply invested I had become in this narrative of power – how to get it and what it would provide.

Our culture is very invested in individual power. We love stories about people pulling themselves up by their bootstraps, succeeding by hard work, application, raw talent. This individualistic lens celebrates and lionizes individual talent so thoroughly that the people who have it are often considered to be above the law, above the social and ethical considerations that constrain the rest of us.

Of course, most of these successes have benefitted mightily from being white, being raised by parents and families with enough wealth and connections to give them an entrée into worlds not available to people of color, or those from less wealthy backgrounds. They are a product of a specific kind of privilege and yet they are celebrated as individuals.

Being part of a community, a group, can be empowering, even if the community doesn't give you entrée into corporate America. Can you think of experiences where you've seen community power? It might be in activism, political action, or organized labor. Having a community behind you, supporting you, can be life affirming and life changing. Have you had that experience?

Physical power and agency

Who has physical power and agency? Depending on how you move through the world, the power of physical strength and agency may be a key consideration in your discernment process. The real impact of ableism in all aspects of life can maintain a power imbalance for anyone with differing abilities or a body size that isn't deemed by the dominant culture to be "acceptable."

A few years ago, chronic pain left me with limited mobility for a few years. After two surgeries in four months, I needed a cane even after I returned to work. I had my handicapped placard, but I quickly realized that didn't help me find parking in downtown Seattle on a workday. It was difficult for me to walk more than a few blocks, so I started leaving extra time to get to any meeting so I could circle around looking for parking.

One day, I found a spot close to where my meeting was, and parked. A young, able-bodied white man came running up to my car and gestured for me to roll down my window.

"This is my spot," he said.

"Excuse me?"

"I need this spot. I'm working at this building, and I have a truck coming and I need to use this spot. You need to move."

I checked to make sure I wasn't in a loading zone. I was not. I gestured to the handicapped placard hanging from my rear-view mirror and held up my cane. "I need to park here to be able to walk to my appointment on this block," I said. I rolled up my window and got out of the car. He started yelling at me, cursing. He was so aggressive that I considered the cane would be useful if he became physical because I could hit him with it. I walked away to my meeting with him still shouting after me. This man had very specific ideas of who had the power to claim that piece of pavement, and it wasn't the woman with the cane and handicapped placard.

Right relationship

Power is like money in that it can be ephemeral, and hard to see. A person who has power in one arena may have none in another. The richest and most powerful oligarchs are still going to die. And we can be just as greedy for power as we can be for money. I've always appreciated the Buddhist concept of "right relationship." This could be a moment for us to consider if we have a right relationship with power.

My understanding of right relationship is that we are engaged as we need to be without grasping or hoarding. A woman goes about her duties as an employed person. That employment may bring her power. She may use that to empower others. Or she might act as a gatekeeper to withhold opportunities from co-workers. There's no fault in getting power through the course of your work or circumstances. The challenge is if you misuse or abuse your power.

Alcoholics and addicts are greedy folks. "For thousands of years we have been demanding more than our share of security prestige and romance. When we seemed to be succeeding, we drank to dream still greater dreams. When we were frustrated, even in part, we drank for oblivion. Never was there enough of what we thought we wanted." (12x12 p 71)

Alcoholics aren't the only ones who get greedy for prestige and power. It's human nature, and something that is encouraged and rewarded in this culture. Social media invites a greed for the power of attention and influence, which is measured by followers or likes or people sharing your content.

It can be useful for us to stop and consider if we are in right relationship to power. Are we slipping into greed? Are we using the power we have to help others? What do you think power will give you? There are many types of power. I've been in situations where having a lawyer gave me access to the legal power to protect myself and my children. Power can protect as well as damage.

Most spiritual practices suggest care around power, money and sex, because as humans we often struggle to stay in right relationship with power, money and sex. Many religious orders take vows of poverty, chastity, and obedience. Being obedient to another means you have less power. It is part of my spiritual curriculum to continue to work to stay in right relationship with power and money, and that takes a lot of vigilance.

Invitation to explore

- What kinds of power do you have? What power do you want, or want more of?

- What do you believe power can get you? Does it protect you? Does it insulate you? Will it corrupt you?

- Is power an individual or community possession? Can you get power by working hard, or is it conferred?

- Who gets to be in power? What do they look like? Do you look like them?

- What confers the most power? Money? Influence? Political clout or elected office? Status within an organization? Family or generational connections? Physical strength or athletic prowess?

- If you have lots of privilege, consider doing a power inventory, and listing the ways in which you have power. Which kinds of power do you take personal credit for, and which do you consider to be part of your inherited privilege? Remember, we can have power in one area and none in another.

Being white gave me lots of power I did nothing to earn in the workplace, even while my gender and status as a single mother reduced my power in other ways.

- Who in your family or community has or had personal power?

- Who has physical power? What kind of experience have you had with physical power or strength? Were you ever overpowered by another? Have you ever used your physical power or strength to intimidate?

- Can you think of an example of a person in public life, your community or family who was a good steward of their power, who used it to help others?

- Can you think of a person who was unskillful in how they wielded power?

- Are there issues of power or influence in your discernment question? What are they?

There's no need to judge yourself. Being ambitious or wanting power can be a motivating force that can be very helpful, especially for people who have lacked power in areas of their life. Plenty of people use their power to help others. Right relationship is a very individual choice and pursuit and can't always be recognized from the outside.

Your Thoughts

CHAPTER SEVENTEEN

Home and Family

Most of us carry narratives around home, family, and caregiving, so it's a useful area of exploration to see which stories limit us and which support us. For those of us who are married, partnered or raising children, this can also be an opportunity to get curious about what narratives are carried by the people we share our homes with, once we are grounded in our own understanding of our stories.

Who takes care of the home? Who takes care of the children? Who takes care of sick family members? Who took care of you? For many of us, this was a woman. Many of the cultural expectations around home, family and caregiving are gendered. Studies show that women who work outside of the home still do more of the chores around the house as well as more childcare than their husband in opposite sex marriages. Even women who earn as much as their husband still do twice the housework he does and two hours more of childcare each week, while he spends three and a half more hours on leisure than she does.[1]

How much should you consider the wants, needs and expectations of your family members when you are making a decision? Since gender roles and cultural expectations can weigh heavily when we are considering a decision, especially one that impacts our family, it's important to get any ideas or narratives out in the light so you can understand what you believe as well as any stories that are no longer relevant for you. As you are considering this, you may want to refer to anything in your values that relates to family.

Parenting

I got married when I was twenty-one, a month before my college graduation. I understand now that I was looking for a pre-made identity, and I thought I had

[1] https://www.npr.org/2023/04/13/1168961388/pew-earnings-gender-wage-gap-housework-chores-child-care

found it in marriage. My father died the summer before my junior year in college. I realized quickly that most of the drive I had to get a career was about my father. I was walking into his narrative of what my career and life should be like. I think if he'd lived, I would have gone to law school, or started to work at a big company. But when he died, I didn't see much point in pursuing grad school or a corporate career because that was something I was doing for him, and now that he was dead it wasn't necessary. I realized that I didn't have a plan of my own. I wanted to be a writer, yes, but the story my father told me about art was that it was valuable, but it wasn't a way to make a living.

By junior year, right after my father's death, the students I went to college with were interviewing for jobs. I remember walking through campus and seeing the signs for recruiters wanting to talk to students, the big-name companies from finance and banking. I had been waiting tables or working in restaurants for most of high school and college, and the thought of deciding what I was going to do as a real job was daunting. I just wanted to write, and had no idea what kind of career I would have to pay the bills.

So, I got married. I had two kids quickly. It was an instant identity. Being a mother is like being in a club with a very visible membership. I didn't realize until I was much older how seductive it was to step into an identity that already existed rather than do the work to figure out my own.

What narratives do you carry about parenting? What stories do you tell yourself about who gets to help parents to parent? The nuclear family with two parents and a few kids has not been a traditional unit for most of our history as human beings. Extended families and communal groups were the norm. Do you have narratives around who *should* watch and raise children? Do you have narratives about day care or children being cared for by paid professionals? Try to understand, without judgement, what expectations the people closest to you have about your family roles as parent, sibling, child. Do you have the same expectations? Where is there conflict?

When I was growing up in the seventies it was not unusual for women to stay home with young children. Now, most families can't afford for one parent to stay home, even to extend the mercilessly short parental leave for a few extra months.

Women who do have that privilege are conflicted about staying home with children. They tell me people keep asking them, "well, what do you *do?*" As if taking care of an infant, a toddler and a home while the breadwinning spouse is out working isn't enough. I still hear people say, "She doesn't work" referring to women who are clearly working; parenting, caregiving, house managing. And I'll correct them, "She doesn't work outside the home."

Our experiences as children can impact our narratives around how we want to be as parents. A man who spent time outdoors with his father in nature as he was growing up may prioritize that in his ideal of fatherhood, since those outings brought him joy he wants to share with his children. A women who grew up with violence in her home may carry stories of how she wants to handle conflict and safety. We may have all sorts of ideas of who we want to be as parents before we have children. I did. Then in the reality of sleepless nights and difficult toddlers I found old wounds resurfacing in a way I didn't expect, which ultimately persuaded me to try therapy.

Who makes decisions?

Many decisions around work or career involve moving to another place or taking on additional responsibilities or hours. Going back to school is expensive and can mean taking on additional debt and reducing income temporarily. Many jobs or artistic pursuits take up time that might have been spent on the family or household, and your partner or children may need to pick up the slack. Certainly, any decision-making process should involve those people who are impacted. But first you should get clear on what you believe you get to ask for when you are part of a family. How do you balance your family's needs with your own in your discernment process? Clearly, this was not something that Ignatius, a Catholic priest, needed to consider.

When I was growing up, we moved often for my father's job. We moved to Los Angeles when I was in ninth grade. I actually made friends there, which didn't happen often. I loved the huge public school I attended. I loved the sun, and the house we had in the canyon with a small pool in the backyard, the smell of eucalyptus and dust. At the end of the summer, our parents told us that we were moving back to Washington DC. They wanted to get us moved back before the school year started. The way I remember it was that we had one day before we left. We found out on a Tuesday that we were leaving on Thursday. One day to pack, to say goodbye to friends in the days before mobile phones or social media. We did a number of these sudden moves over the years. The movers would come in and pack up everything as we left it. I'd be unpacking in a new city and in a box full of paper I'd find the carefully wrapped leavings on my bedside table from my last day in the old house. A water glass. A rock from the beach. A pack of tissues and a highlighter pen. My life in the old town frozen and wrapped in paper and packed up in cardboard boxes and shipped on a truck to another place. We lived in Los Angeles for less than a year.

My sister and I were never involved in the conversations about where and when we moved. My parents weren't democratic; when I was allowed to shave my legs or get my ears pierced were all part of a carefully coded set of timelines my mother sporadically communicated. It would never have occurred to me that my sister or I would be consulted about moving. Which I still think is valid. When the main breadwinner needs to make a move to continue to support the family, that's a priority. But this move could have been done in a way that allowed me more time to process the transition and say goodbye to my friends.

Who gets to make decisions in a family? What criteria are prioritized as they decide? How do you navigate a situation where your decisions will impact others? For example, taking a new job that will require you to move to another city and uproot your two teenaged children who are resistant to leaving their friends. What if one of your children is especially talented and moving to a new city will give them the opportunity to pursue their talent, be it artistic or athletic? What about the other children who don't want to leave?

I have friends, a husband and wife who have been married for many years, who take turns making career decisions that involve a move. Her turn, then his turn. It is useful to have a way of making decisions in a family or criteria set before you have to actually make one of those big decisions. The earlier exercises on values and your navigational cues may be useful here. Bring those out, and have discussions with your family. Can you include their values in the exercise? Can you negotiate where feasible? Can parents take turns making big decisions so each has time to prioritize their needs, or can a child who has to relocate go visit her friends in the summertime for a few weeks?

Family issues and conflict around change can be some of the most fraught we encounter in decision making. Even when you are grounded in what you want, what your values and priorities are, you may run into resistance from your family and loved ones. I've found outside help to be useful in these cases; family therapy, couples counseling, or individual psychotherapy are sometimes necessary to navigate these kinds of conflict.

Who takes care of the parents?

What do you believe you are responsible for when it comes to caring for disabled, sick or elderly parents or siblings? Who takes care of family members, especially aging parents? This can be especially complex when time and money are tight. Managing a parent's healthcare needs is always difficult, but it is especially so in the American healthcare system for people who are not wealthy. What do you owe your parents and other siblings if you have them?

Aging parents can be uncooperative. It's hard to manage a parent's finances when Mom or Dad isn't ready to give up access to their bank accounts, even when they've been scammed or lost money through avoidable mistakes. On the other hand, I've seen competent aging parents with adult children who want to dictate what financial decisions a parent should make as if their future inheritance already belonged to the children and was no longer the parent's money to manage and spend.

Given the complexity of questions about who cares for elderly relatives, it can be difficult to get the space and quiet to decide what is right for you if you are facing a decision that might change your availability to be a caregiver. Especially if you make a decision that your parents or family don't agree with, or that requires others to step up in a way they might not want to, like the sibling who doesn't want to help even though they can and has left you holding the proverbial bag for years. Sometimes we make decisions about what is best for our lives that people in our family don't approve of, decisions that go against familiar, cherished scripts.

I was estranged from my mother for most of the last fifteen years of her life. Lots of people, in and out of my family, thought I should have a relationship with my mother. They were often religious people who cited the commandment to honor your father and mother. For years I would try to enumerate all the bad things my mother had done to me to justify why I stepped away. But I didn't want to stay in that victim stance, or rehash negative stories, so I stopped trying to explain my decision to others. I was always surprised how people who hardly knew me could have such vehement opinions on what they thought my relationship with a woman they had never met should look like.

We can allow people to experience the consequences of their choices. Whether that's an addicted person who gets incarcerated, or a profligate parent who needs to live in reduced circumstances in old age, or a healthy adult child who needs to move out of her parent's house and get a job. They won't like it. We may have a range of emotions about their experience, but we also don't need to rush in and save everyone.

That's a hard one for people from a religious background, whether they still practice or not. The commandment to honor your father and mother did not, for me, mean saving my mother from the consequences of her choices. But it did mean not talking trash about her to every person I met to explain why I didn't have anything to do with her anymore.

On the other hand, I have friends who have cared for difficult parents to the end of the parent's life and found it to be a deeply healing and life-giving experience. Others care for cherished parents at the end of life with tenderness and commitment as an expression of their love and gratitude to that parent, and their stories of Mom or Dad on their deathbed are filled with connection and even joy.

Making decisions that are best for you can be challenging, especially when you aren't showing up in the way that your family and culture think you should be. Which is why leaning into this intentional process of discernment can help. I made my decisions about what kind of relationship I wanted with my mother intentionally, over time, with discernment, and with the input of wise and spiritual people. And I have never regretted those decisions.

The role of caregiver

Taking on the role of the caregiver and dependable one can give us a sense of identity and satisfaction. It could be the role you've filled your whole life and everyone in your family expects it of you. You might be in a caring profession like medicine and find people turning to you for advice outside of work. Many choose that role and are fulfilled by it. But what if you're not fulfilled, or want to be a nurse or therapist at your job and not with your family? What if you never asked for the role of caregiver, or want to move on from that?

Being a single mother was a big part of my identity. I'm proud that I was able to support my kids. But when my daughter left for college, it took me a long time to learn how to do things for myself, how to rebalance my life without the intense needs of raising a family. I took very quick showers when my children were young and it became a habit. Even though I have plenty of hot water and could stay in the shower as long as I want I'm still in and out in a short period of time, still operating on the script that young children may be wreaking havoc outside the door.

Generally, what we do serves us in some way. If there is a behavior or pattern around family that no longer serves you, why do you do it? I'm thinking specifically around parenting or caregiving. I've asked myself that same question, and answered the way you might: "I do it because there isn't anyone else to do it." Which is valid and true.

However, sometimes we do it because we have old narratives that tell us we must. An elderly friend of mine was caring for her equally elderly husband, because he was ill and needed care that she could provide. He was not always kind to her. For a while, she put up with it, because of stories she carried about gender roles and her obligation to the man to whom she had been married for decades. It didn't occur to her that she had options, until she reexamined those stories. She continued to care for him, but set clear boundaries around what kind of behavior she would and would not accept and what help she was going to get a home health aide to provide, even though he didn't want care from anyone but his wife. She was able to do this because she gained clarity around what stories were getting in the way of her taking care of herself while still taking care of her husband.

Home as a physical space

For many people, the physical space where they live has deep significance. They might be especially attached to a particular aesthetic that connects them to their culture or community. They may consider their home to be a retreat from the world and want it to be orderly and clean. One person may relish living in a city, another may feel lost if they aren't close to a body of water. A particular location may be important because family or friends are nearby. Where to live, who cares for the home, and what that home represents for the people who live there can cause conflict in some couples or families.

Many decisions can impact where and how we live, quite literally. In many places, home ownership is too expensive for most people. I grew up with a narrative that home ownership was critical to financial stability. My friend Juliette, who grew up in New York City, totally disagreed. "Why would you want to own a house? I want to be able to call the super to fix anything that breaks, and move whenever I want," she said.

What stories do you have about home? It could be narratives around buying or renting, about moving often or staying put. It could be narratives about how clean your house should be and who does that cleaning, or where you want to raise a family or retire.

Invitation to explore

Parenting and caregiving

- Did your family have rules, spoken or unspoken, about who the caregivers were? Sit quietly for a moment, close your eyes, and think of the word "caregiver." Who comes to mind?

- For those of you who are parents or considering being parents, what narratives do you have around parenting? How are/were these influenced by your experience as a child? How did your understanding of parenting change after you had children?

- Consider the full range of the parenting experience, from feeding an infant in the middle of the night to who takes the child to doctor's appointments, to who stays home from work with a sick kid. Are these gendered? If you have a co-parent, it might be useful to discuss these questions with them – not to judge, but to get curious about what existing maps, assumptions or stories might be operating beneath the surface.

- What stories come up for you about who makes money and how and if that impacts their responsibilities as a parent and partner? Do you believe there should be different expectations for the primary breadwinner?

- Are there other family members or caregivers who could help take over responsibilities you think are yours alone? Where your choices might impact someone in your family and you believe you have an ethical, moral or relational duty, can you consider practical alternatives? If you've been the sibling who lives nearest to Dad and takes him to doctor's appointments and you want to go to grad school out of town, are there other family members or people in the community who can fill in once you move?

- What kind of sibling/parent/child do you want to be? Imagine that you are at the end of your life. Consider either side of the decision you are making, think of each of the potential outcomes. Do you think there is one you will regret more?

Making family decisions

- When you consider the decision that you are making, who will be impacted? Write down a list of people in your family who will be affected and how. For each person impacted, what do you think you are allowed to do or not do?

- Look back at your family, community, neighborhood. Who made decisions about the family, and how were they made? Was it talked about or decided by fiat? Were children heard and did they get to participate? Or was it only the adults? Or only one of the adults? What do you think of that – was it right?

- Did you have experiences as a child where an adult made a decision that impacted the family? Perhaps it was a move for a new job, or choosing to leave a marriage. What did you learn from that experience? Does it still impact you?

- Were there big family decisions that were made for motives that were not financial or career oriented; say one parent wanted to move to be closer to family, or to be in a different climate, or to pursue opportunities not connected to work, like an arts fellowship?

Home

- What is the role and importance of your physical space, the place where you live? Do you want to rent or own? What is feasible given where you live and your life stage? Does that play into your decision at all?

- Do these topics bring any new information or energy to your discernment question?

Your Thoughts

CHAPTER EIGHTEEN

Voice

Who gets to speak? Who should remain silent? Many of us carry stories about who is allowed to get noticed or hold forth or take center stage. These can be supportive or limiting narratives, and possibly relevant for you to examine, especially if you are discerning a question that involves having a voice, using it, being the center of attention, centering your experience, or speaking up for others.

The last time I remember using my voice fully and unselfconsciously was when I was about thirteen years old. I was visiting my grandmother Frances, which made me happy. It was a sunny summer day, and I was walking down the long staircase from her deck to the street below. I was alone, and I was happy, and I sang a song. I remember how strong I felt, how my voice opened up and felt like an instrument, and it all connected, my breath, my body, the song. It was a supremely joyful moment.

Then I heard mean, mocking laughter. A trio of teenagers was walking along the street below. I hadn't seen them, I thought I was alone. They laughed at me, and one of the boys mocked me. I couldn't see their faces. I just heard the derision floating up the stairs. I stopped singing. I was a new teen, so awkward under the best of circumstances, and I felt their mocking laughter the way I felt the sting of nettles in the woods; persistent, leaving marks.

My mother's family had lots of singers. And Frances had lots of energy around who could sing and when. My great aunt Marjorie was an opera singer. When I knew her, she was almost blind and wore thick glasses with green tinted lenses. But old photographs showed her on opera stages in Europe, in long gowns. In old age her hair was still blonde, and she still wore it piled up on her head, the way she had when she was on those stages. Marjorie would put on a record of an opera – usually La Bohème or La Traviata – and sing her favorite arias. I didn't know much about the music, but I remember the quality of her voice. It was beautiful and arresting, with a rich warmth. She spoke many languages, and lived in Mexico City. When she sang, Frances, her sister, would cry. Which made sense to me.

My aunt Margo was a blues singer. Her voice was also arresting, a smoky contralto. She was beautiful, and when she sang for us in the living room, her voice filled the room, a surprisingly large voice from someone with such a small frame. My mother had a quieter voice, and automatically sang harmony to her sisters' melody. My mother liked to sing, she played the guitar and sang the folk songs of the 60s and 70s. She would sing for my grandmother. I knew the songs and as a little kid I would sing along, but Frances would shush me so she could hear my mother.

It hurt my feelings that Frances wanted me to be quiet. I was a child, I thought of singing as something we all did together, like we did at school, or on car trips. Frances said my grandfather, her husband Joe, used to sing with Bing Crosby, that they were friends and sang together. That was important to her – it wasn't just that he knew Bing Crosby, he *sang* with him. I don't ever remember Frances singing outside of church, but she loved listening to the singing of others. I think she had a narrative that singing was a performance, not a participatory sport, and it was done by people who were good at it, and she was not one of the people who was good at it. Maybe having a sister who was an opera singer made her feel that way.

The narrative that you have to be expert to speak up is pervasive. Who confers that expert badge? We don't have to look far for voices that were unexpected when they were first heard; think of singers and artists who didn't achieve recognition at first because the sounds they made challenged the status quo, or people in marginalized communities whose art was ignored, scorned or stolen and imitated by artists from the dominant group. Our culture has very specific ideas about who has the right to be on a stage. A friend of mine is an expert in her field, and often gives presentations on stages. She describes herself as fat. She is careful about how she dresses to speak in public, but she says that for the first ten minutes of any talk all anyone sees is a fat woman on stage. Then they get over their surprise and listen to her. I've often heard Black people be congratulated by white people on how "articulate" they are when speaking in public, even if they have a JD, MD, PhD or other letters clustered behind their names. The cultural freight around who gets to talk, and where and how they get to speak is significant, for some more than others.

I have given many trainings about how to give presentations in a corporate setting. I pay lots of attention to voices and how people use their voices. I notice when women go up at the end of sentences even when they aren't asking a question, or talk from the back of their throats like they don't want to project too much. They might speak softly, or with a higher voice or a childish almost lisp. All of those are ways that women give away power in a work setting. I can usually tell which is innate and which learned, but I at least want women to understand what they are communicating when they distort their natural voices to conform with gendered expectations. I'm not talking about natural variations – clearly there are people who have high voices. I'm talking about a woman who speaks in the normal range when we're both pouring out coffee, but when she is in front of a group she kicks into a higher register and her consonants get softer. I've done it, felt my voice shift to better meet expectations in a personal or professional setting, before I even realize what I'm doing. When I start those presentation trainings, I say that getting feedback on how you talk can be very uncomfortable, and that anyone can opt out or stop whenever they want to, because these are all opt in, optional trainings. Thinking about how you use your own voice right now might bring up discomfort. And it's ok to opt out or pause here if that's the case.

Using your voice is bigger than just how you speak. Being an artist, having an opinion, asking for what you want, setting boundaries, advocating for yourself or a loved one – all of these are ways to use your voice. We can use our voices singly, as soloists, or we can be part of a group, in a choir. Both have satisfactions and challenges.

Invitation to explore

- Think of your actual voice. Do you like it? The trope is that absolutely everyone hates the sound of their own voice when they hear a recording of themselves. In fact, the sound of my own voice is my one unalloyed vanity. I like my own voice. It feels mellow, smart, electric. I can hear every cigarette I ever smoked, and I like the sound of them. What do you like about your voice?

- Think back on your family. Who was allowed to talk? When and why? Is there anyone who had a distinctive voice – either their presence/perspective or their actual voice itself?

- Did your family sing or make music? Did people read aloud? Who led the singing or reading? Was it communal or individual?

- Were you part of a faith tradition that involved preaching? Who preached? Who sang during worship services? Who didn't?

- Who was silenced? Were there family members or people in your community who were not allowed to talk? Why? How did they react?

- Consider any ways in which you use your voice differently in different spaces and why. That might be code switching, or literally altering how you use your vocal cords in certain situations.

- Did anyone in your family or community use their voice to bully or dominate? It could be a person who was often angry or loud, or someone who took over conversations or told everyone else what to do, or acted like they were the authority on everything. How has that impacted you? Did you speak louder to be heard, or did you stay quiet to avoid conflict, or to demonstrate that you aren't like that person?

- What language was spoken in your home? Was it the same language spoken in your community? The larger geographical area? Were there languages or accents that were considered "better" or "worse" for you, your family or community? Do you have positive or negative associations with a specific language? Was your community historically denied their language or punished for using it?

- If you are in an immigrant family, is there a divide between who speaks the language of the place where your family came from? Do you feel like your understanding of that first language isn't good enough, that you should be more fluent? My father understood Italian, but only responded in English to his older relatives. He didn't teach his daughters any Italian, he wanted us to be American. I wish I had learned Italian as a child.

- Did anyone in your family or community who had less power get to talk? Were children invited into conversations? Did they get to have opinions and express them? How were people treated who had trouble talking, because of a stutter or disability?

- When you watch television or films, do people who look like you get to speak? Do they get center stage, meaty roles, significant character development? Does that play into cultural narratives that impact you?

- Many people dislike public speaking or any type of performance. Do you? Can you think of any times where you spoke up and commanded attention? What was that like?

- Have you ever had any trouble with your voice? Do you get sick and lose your voice, literally? When you're nervous, does it hit your throat? Do you have the sensation of choking? Do you often clear your throat, as if something is caught in there, even when you're not ill?

- Can you think of a time when you used your voice fully? Maybe you were shouting in anger, or singing loudly, or calling out the answer to a question in a game night. How did that feel? Did it surprise you? Delight you?

- What did other people tell you about your voice? Were you told you talked too quickly? Too softly? Too loudly? Was anyone surprised that you had talent, or were intelligent? Did anyone ever mock you for speaking or using your voice, or for an accent or the way you spoke? What impact did that have on you?

- Is there anything that has arisen for you during this exercise that could relate to or influence the decision you are discerning?

Your Thoughts

CHAPTER NINETEEN

Spirituality

Does your spirituality or spiritual practice support your decision-making process? Do you have narratives about spirituality that help or hinder tapping into a deep stream of truth? I have, for most of my career, hidden the fact that I have a spiritual life and spiritual practice. Conservative Christianity has tainted the word Christian, leaving little cultural space for my progressive beliefs. I hate the caveats. "I'm Christian but . . ." I think every person should be able to get the health care they need, including gender affirming care, reproductive care and abortion. We are all made and loved by the Divine, in all our variety and difference, whether we are gay, straight, trans, cis. Women can and should be equal leaders in any secular or church community, which means ordination as deacons, priests, and bishops. Our society should aid and support the poor, the sick, the refugees, the unhoused. The caveats are exhausting.

Clearly, my beliefs deviate from many of the Catholics I grew up with, and Catholics in my family. I go to an Episcopal Church now, because their beliefs are more in line with mine. But Catholic traditions, especially the mystic tradition and Jesuit spirituality, have deepened and enriched my life, and are foundational to my discernment process. So, for those of you who have a spiritual practice or are open to that idea, here are some things to consider. Do you believe people can have a purpose or calling? Do you believe that your relationship with the Divine or your Higher Power can be a two-way relationship? Can you get guidance from a source larger than you? How can you tap into that source?

Calling

I believe that we each have a purpose, which is demonstrated to us by what we love. The God I understand shows us what we are meant to do by giving us a deep love for the doing of it. Sometimes you can see this in a person very early. The violinist Yehudi Menuhin was a child prodigy. He was given a toy violin for his fourth birthday. "I burst into sobs, threw it on the ground, and would have nothing more to do with it," Menuhin said. His talent, his calling, demanded a real violin to express what was inside him.

"Vocation" is commonly used to talk about someone who is "called" to religious life as nun or priest. Too often people think being called to a vocation means God demanding that you do something you don't want to do. The people I know who are called to be nuns or priests are generally joyful about it, but in the cultural narrative a call to religious life is often considered to be unpleasant. After all, who would rejoice in celibacy, poverty or obedience, the standard vows for Christian religious life?

I invite you to reframe your narratives around calling. As Howard Thurman said, "Don't ask what the world needs. Ask what makes you come alive, and go do it. Because what the world needs is people who have come alive." What you are meant to do is what brings you to life, where you are the most yourself. You may or may not make money from that thing, it may be true work and not econ, but it can be a steadfast companion throughout your life. Finding what it is you were made to do is as deeply joyful as finding true love or a best friend. Of course, there may be more than one thing, and that thing may change over time. But the sense of coming home, of direction and purpose can be very satisfying.

I believe in a God who will give me guidance. I can ask a question and I will get answers. I might not like the answers, and they may not come to me in any direct way. But I'll get guidance. Ignatius used the process which became his Spiritual Exercises to get that guidance, to understand how to best serve God. I find this process to be most fruitful when we connect the decision we are trying to make to the calling we hear.

Do you have a calling? I invite you to think of calling very broadly. One person may have a deep desire to help the earth, and work to stop plastics pollution in the ocean. Another person may believe strongly that they want to help children with mental health issues. These individuals may have no spiritual practice or tradition, but I would call that deep sense of mission a kind of calling.

How do you recognize a sense of calling, if it's not a term you're familiar with, or if it is too bound up in religious language to be something you've considered before? Many of the questions in this book which you may have considered up to this point are clues to your calling. What did you love when you were a child? What fascinated you? What delights you now? What do you believe strongly and prioritize in your life? What causes or issues do you support? What do your values tell you about what is important to you?

I remember a friend in college who wanted to be a doctor. We both worked hard, we'd spend many weekend nights at the library studying. I thought pre-med was just her major, that being a doctor was a way for her to earn a living. When I first saw her with patients, during her training, it was clear this was her calling. She had always wanted to be a doctor, and when I saw her in a hospital hallway, crouched down next to a patient in a wheelchair, her hand on his arm, looking into his face and listening, I saw quite clearly that this was what she was meant to do. This was her calling. There was a kind of light coming from her, and that patient was basking in it. She's been a physician for years.

In my experience, a calling is a lot like being in love with a place. There's a beach we used to go to when I was a kid and I loved it. I would think about it when I wasn't there; how the tide flats smelled at low tide, the taste of marshmallows toasted over a fire of driftwood, going out on the boat with my grandfather and uncle and picking up the crab pots and cooking the crab for dinner, using the end of a crab leg to pick out the sweet meat of the big front claws. The long days of summer in northern Washington State, where dusk stretches past ten at night. I longed to go there, luxuriated when I was there, and missed it when I left. You may travel or live other places, but there can be a place that is lodged in your heart. A calling is like that, you are homesick for it when you are away, and at home when you are there.

A calling can make you restless, unsettled, or demanding, like Menuhin as a toddler destroying the toy violin. When you're not doing what it is you are called to do your life can feel flat, pointless. It's like a black and white movie. Then when you do whatever it is you were meant to do, everything is in color, saturated, deep. When I write, I often feel a rich peace, and time moves differently – hours can pass and I won't be aware of the time at all. Others might feel grounded, or competent, or they might stop thinking about themselves altogether, and become fully unselfconscious.

Often, we are preoccupied with the calling. A person who is called to music may be interested in music beyond the point where others see it as a hobby or interest and almost think of it as an obsession. You're not only following the creations of another person or people, you want to create, you want to be active and involved in that passion. Is there something you can't not do? How might that be considered in your discernment process?

A calling doesn't need to be big or dramatic, or even something that is recognized by those around us. People can be called to baking or caring for animals, to creating gardens or providing hospitality, to travel or accounting or building cabinets. What is it that makes you feel alive?

Reciprocity

I really believe that if you are trying to help the universe, the universe helps back. I call it reciprocity. I use this term with clients who aren't spiritual but who have a deep sense of mission. And when I say it, they know exactly what I mean. The sense that sometimes things just come together – a lucky chance, a fortuitous meeting, an unexpected insight. That's reciprocity, when the universe meets you and helps you.

Usually, a calling benefits others. Most people who have a calling can connect it to a benefit to something larger than themselves. They are helping their family, community, the earth, a school or political system, a workplace and the other people who are there. They may create jobs or opportunity or build things. Artists create beauty and provoke or surprise. Teachers educate.

Many people believe that if they are doing work to help their God, whatever that might be, their God will assist and support them. They believe they get support in very direct ways, like a fortuitous job opportunity or unexpected legal ruling or financial windfall. For others the support is subtler, spiritual energy or sustenance, or a sense of clarity. I believe that support is available to people who don't believe in God as well. If you can tap into a sense of mission or a deeper meaning in your decision making, it can open you up to reciprocity.

What, exactly, is reciprocity? My hope is that as you figure out what you are called to do to help yourself, your family, your community, or the world, you will open up a channel to reciprocity. And then something will happen – the unexpected assist, the intuitive insight, the serendipitous meeting – and you will stop and think, wait, that's reciprocity, that thing she wrote about just actually happened!

There's a Jewish concept that over every blade of grass angels are saying "grow, grow." Many faith traditions believe that the Divine is in the world; in us, in nature. Why shouldn't the Divine also be whispering "grow, grow" over us as we try to do what we believe is our calling?

I know there are people who like the idea of manifesting. They wish for something to happen; they state affirmations about a desired outcome. And they may get what they manifest. I understand how the concept of being able to manifest a specific outcome provides a sense of power and validation. Reciprocity is different. In manifesting, you are asking for something desired and helping yourself believe you deserve it or can make it happen. With reciprocity, you aren't asking for a specific thing to happen. You are opening yourself up to new information, insight or experiences and waiting to see what it is. We'll return to this in the next section, but here's what it looks like for me.

I'm writing this book because I have a calling to be a writer, and I think the book should be in the world. As I write about discernment, I am discerning what should be in the book about discernment. This morning, I was struggling with the writing. I ran into a friend who is a writer. I wasn't intending to talk about the book, but I did, and as we talked a few things fell into place for me. I received new information. It was unexpected, serendipitous, the two of us sitting in the summer sun talking about writing. I think if I walk through the world asking a question, people, situations, and experiences will come into my life that help me answer the question. Sometimes by closing a door or removing an option. Other times by putting a book or podcast or idea in my path. The point is that I'm looking, open-minded, with the question close to the surface. My friend and I are in community together, which helps me be open. I have let myself be known here and she knows I'm writing a book. I know she is a writer, an accomplished journalist. When she asked me how the writing was going, I could tell her, and stay open and curious in listening to her response.

Most of us are like a person walking around a city looking at their phone. Let's imagine a man named Roger. Roger knows where he is going, but only has a small part of his awareness on his surroundings, because he's looking at his phone. He's not going to trip over a curb or walk into the street, but he is also going to miss the tree covered in white blooms like bunches of grapes, or the new puppy in his neighbor's front yard or the man across the street walking hand in hand with a toddler as she sings a song in Spanish. He may also miss the neighbor who is pulling out the same weed Roger has struggled with using a new tool that would have solved Roger's weed problem, if he had only looked up and seen it being used. By not taking time to notice a worker putting a solar panel on a roof, Roger didn't have the train of thought that challenged him to put more action behind his commitment to helping the planet.

Discernment is putting down your phone and walking through your neighborhood curious and open to whoever you are going to meet, and taking it all in with the confidence that you will get the answers you need.

Colloquy

I've met many people who believe in God and are part of a faith tradition, but don't believe in a personal God, a Divine entity who cares about them as individuals. If you don't believe in God, if that's not how you see the world, that's one thing. But I feel bad for people who believe in God but don't think that God is interested in them or cares about them.

Throughout the Spiritual Exercises, Ignatius suggests we have a "colloquy" with the Divine. Jesus, Mary, God, whatever calls to us. "The colloquy is made by speaking exactly as one friend speaks to another." (SE #54)

What would you say to the Divine if you believed that the Divine was interested in everything you have to say? I think about how much I love my grandchildren. Everything they do is interesting to me. Their observations of the world, how they react to loud noises or surprises, how they learn and move. I am fascinated by them. What if the Divine is equally fascinated and in love with you?

One of the powerful messages in both the Spiritual Exercises and the Twelve Steps is that there is a process to clear away whatever blocks us from the love of God. We don't have to do anything to get the love of God. We don't get it for being good, or wise, or kind or spiritual. Sometimes we can't see it or feel it because it's just not our path yet. At other times, something might be blocking us; fear or contempt prior to investigation, or inordinate attachments. Or God may be obscured by an accumulation of stories that aren't true for us. By connecting with the Divine, we can access a source of power and wisdom and guidance. "We ask God in prayer and meditation for guidance on each specific matter and the right answer will come if we want it." (BB p. 69) And, yes, you can get guidance and power from God without believing in God. Your belief or lack of belief in God doesn't stop God from loving you and whispering "grow, grow."

I'm going to break the Invitation to Explore into three sections. You might want to read them all and see if anything resonates unexpectedly. As always, if something doesn't resonate or you feel aversion to it, move on. Rest where you find fruit.

Invitations to explore

If you're ok with the God thing

- Do you believe that the Divine loves you? Is interested in you? Can give you guidance? Have you had experiences of that happening in your life? Have you known others who have?

- What if, like Bill Wilson writes, you can pick your own idea of the Divine? Take a paper and draw a line down the middle. On one side write down every attribute of God that you believe right now or carry from your youth. Is God male? Judging? Aloof? A figment of imagination? A fairy tale? On the other side write what you would like your Higher Power to be. Real, kind, compassionate. Is there anything from the first list you'd like to get rid of? Anything from the second list you'd like to include in your understanding of the Divine?

- How does the Divine give you guidance? Is it through scripture? Teaching? Other people? Art? Nature? Can you get it directly or do you need an intermediary? How do you know for sure it's from God? Do you have a spiritual advisor or trusted elder you talk to about God?

- Have you ever felt called? What were you called to do or be? Did that turn out to be true and life giving to you, or did you later understand that differently?

- Ignatius wrote frequently of having a colloquy, or conversation, with the Divine. He also suggests "asking for what you desire" in this process. That may be wisdom, patience, perseverance, understanding, whatever would support you. As for who you talk to, I invite you to think broadly about which aspect of the Divine you are addressing and use whatever appeals to you – a Saint, Jesus, Mary, Ganesh, Gaia, Spirit. Have a conversation about what you desire. Use your senses. Imagine who you are talking to and their receptive interest in you. Pause to listen to see if they talk back. How does that feel for you?

If you're curious about the God thing

- Try the exercise above about writing down what God is or could be for you and what you would like God to be. What comes up for you? This might be easier for people who aren't sure about God than those who are or once were.

- Can you think of a time when you felt a connection to the numinous, to something greater? It might be in nature, or in love, with the birth of a child or the peaceful death of an elder. It might be awe at a piece of art, or music, or architecture. It could be in scientific work, marveling at the complexity of creation. Have you ever felt this, even for a fleeting moment? What do you take from that?

- Consider the idea that there is a Higher Power who loves you and is trying to get through to you, throwing proverbial pebbles at the window of your mind. Was the Divine in any of those moments of awe?

- What works against your belief in God? It may be all the bad things that happen in the world – how could a loving God allow that to happen? It could be old injuries from religions in your youth, or the way people can try to use an idea of God to harm others. Do you have experiences with people who believed in God but struggled with these same questions? Do you believe doubt and faith can peacefully co-exist or even deepen one another?

- Ask the Divine to show up. Then pay attention and see what happens. After my son died, I started having unexpected interactions with birds. I wanted God to show up as birds. I wanted to be reminded that there was another kind of energy, another place, something outside of the abyss of grief. And birds showed up. One Christmas morning there were over a dozen red robins outside in my small front yard. That may have nothing to do with God, but it was unusual, unexpected, and deeply comforting.

- Have you ever felt called? What was that like? Did it turn out, in retrospect, to be true or life giving or useful?

If you don't believe in the God thing

- First of all, I'm glad you're here, and glad you're still reading.

- What is your moral and ethical code and how was it developed? Does it have any similarities with any faith traditions? Are there ways in which it is superior to particular faith traditions? For example, there are faith traditions that don't talk much about stewardship of the earth, and you may have an ethical framework that prioritizes care of the planet, and that value may be the lens through which you make decisions about everything from how you travel to what you eat.

- Does the idea of reciprocity appeal to you? Could it be true? Have you ever had an experience that might fit that concept?

- Have you ever felt called or drawn to something or someone? What was that experience like for you?

- What do you believe in? Science, care for the world, a particular political or economic system? Do these beliefs help or influence you in your discernment process?

See what comes up for you and how it might influence your decision-making process. Note that there will be specific practice instructions for connecting with a Higher Power in Chapter 25 The Intuitive Thought.

Your Thoughts

CHAPTER TWENTY

Rest

As I write this, I have a cold. I've been up coughing over the last few nights, which leaves me exhausted during the day. Waking up in the morning is a slog until I get the first pot of tea into me. I've been sick for about a week, which seems like way too long. For a few days I lost my voice, which was a challenge as I tried to get through an executive coaching session with a client while speaking in a cracked whisper.

I don't do rest well. Even when I'm ill, I don't give myself permission to just sit, drink tea, get well. If I am forced to limit my activity, I become restive and guilty. Who gets to rest? What does rest mean? How should we prioritize rest as we make life decisions?

When I was in high school, I did sports and had a part time job. It was a demanding academic schedule with two to three hours of homework every night and on the weekends. I was stressed out about getting into a good college, and gathered extra-curricular activities like merit badges. Once, I looked at my schedule and realized the only times I could rest were moments in class. Only in class could I just listen and take notes, without having to produce anything. That wasn't a healthy way to live. My father was very ill, the family dynamics were challenging. Doing well in school was something that I could do, and it made me feel like I was in control. It's not surprising that high school was where I began to drink heavily. I justified my weekend binge drinking because I needed a break after all the work I did. It never occurred to me to work less, to drop a sport or an AP class.

As an adult, I rarely took vacations. The only time I took off from work was after I was fired and received a settlement or severance. Which happened multiple times. On those occasions I would take a month or two off. I called them sabbaticals. And I rested. I didn't literally sleep, but I took it easy. I spent more time with my kids, I gardened, and I wrote. Those were always restorative times, and I look back on them with fondness. Those months stand out in my recollection much more than the years in which I worked fifty or sixty hours a week. I don't remember those jobs; they are just a bundled blur of planes and conference rooms and interminable meetings. But I remember planting roses in the house where we used to live, and being home in the afternoon when the kids returned from school.

As you decide whatever it is you are considering, are you factoring in rest? As you imagine your new direction, are you being realistic about the rest you will need? It might be a period of rest each day or an extended break after a project or class. I have taken jobs or planned schedules that left me no days off, working grueling hours. When my children were little, after the divorce, I worked three jobs, seven days a week. I try not to do that now. This can be especially challenging for artists, who have work and econ to balance, which can feel like two full time jobs, or those with caregiving or parenting responsibilities.

Rest can and should be built into the busiest schedule. You might not be able to get a vacation or even a day off, but you could fit in a bubble bath.

As we discussed in Chapter 8 about the Two Standards, anything that works against our innate physical, spiritual and psychological needs is dangerous and, as Ignatius says, "the deadly enemy of our human nature." (SE #136).

Rest for you may be a reasonable work schedule, or time for vacations or retreats or time alone in the day or whatever is restorative to you. Rest may mean factoring in recovery time after something difficult; a month off after taking the Bar Exam, or a three-week trip when your divorce is final, or saving enough for an extra month of parental leave before you have to return to work after having a baby.

Rest may be having realistic expectations of yourself. I took more time than I thought I would need after major surgery, because I didn't heal as quickly as the doctors said I would. I wish I had chosen to take more time off after my son died. In America where we have such limited paid sick time, maternity leave or bereavement leave, it's easy to believe the voices insisting that you must be productive at times when productivity isn't possible or appropriate. Capitalism tells us we are units of production, not human beings who get sick, and bleed, and grieve, who give birth and age and get hurt. We need to fight for the space and time to sleep, recuperate, heal.

And I understand that the less privilege you have, the less likely you are to be able to make that space. When I was taking care of my son at home after his brain injury, I was chronically exhausted. Not because I wasn't managing my schedule or considering my need for rest. It was because there was quite literally no one to help me care for him except for my teenaged daughter. Sometimes life is just hard, and you can't rest the way you would wish. Try not to judge yourself if your life circumstances preclude the kind of rest you'd like to have, that you need. But keep it in mind when you get or ask for a break. Are you taking advantage of any times you're free to just rest? Or are you, like me, filling the time with chores and busyness?

Rest is a component of a balanced life, and we should make sure that we are considering and accounting for our need to rest when we make any decision.

Invitation to Explore

- What narratives do you have about rest and relaxation? Did the stories come from your family, your community, your education or past work experience?

- Do you ever nap, meditate, take a few moments to rest your eyes? Have you ever done those things? What narratives do you have about taking a break in the day to sleep, meditate or just rest?

- If you already have a career, what is the expectation for time spent at work? Is that realistic or healthy for you? Would you consider it to be realistic and healthy for most people? In advertising and technology, the fields I know most about, the expectation is long hours, especially around a new product launch or a pitch. Rarely did I work a forty-hour work week, it was always more. Do you work in a career or corporate culture that has unrealistic expectations of how much you work, or how you should be available outside of work? For example, medical training is notorious for inhumane schedules.

- Do you get vacation time? Do you take vacation time? This could be a three-day weekend staycation or a month-long tour of another country. Are the vacations you are able to afford now your ideal? If not, what would your ideal be?

- Do leaders and people in your organization take vacation time? Is the cultural expectation at your job or career that you must be available on vacation or break, checking emails, being on call in some way? Or is the culture one in which unplugging completely from work when ill or on vacation is the norm?

- What narratives do you have about vacations and work? Do you think that people will take over your job if you're gone for a long vacation? Or do you believe that a solid break from work helps refresh and reenergize a person?

- When do you turn off work or personal notifications on your devices for email or social media? Every night when you sleep? During the evenings when you're with your family? On the weekends? Vacations? Is this your ideal? If not, what would your ideal be?

- Can you look at your family or friends and think of someone who had or has what you now consider to be a good work/life/rest balance? What was or is their schedule?

- When you are ill, do you rest? Do you take sick days if you have them? If yes, then how does that feel for you? If no, why not?

- How many hours a night do you sleep? Is that enough for you? Do you have any health or emotional issues because of lack of sleep?

- If you don't prioritize rest in a way that your circumstances support, do you know why? I've used work and busyness to push away difficult emotions, or to assuage insecurities by congratulating myself on how productive or useful or invaluable I've been. If you don't rest, and more rest would be feasible or possible, how does that serve you?

- Can you see a way that the decision you are making could support or limit a healthy balance of rest and work in your life?

- Does anything that you are realizing about your relationship with rest impact the decision you are making?

Your Thoughts

CHAPTER TWENTY-ONE

Seasons

When my kids were young, people would frequently tell me that they grow up so quickly. It was always an older person who said this, looking down at my two young children, a wistful greed in their eyes, remembering. "They grow up so fast! You blink your eyes and they're grown." I remember thinking, ruefully, that I wouldn't mind fast forwarding through parts of this.

People in community measure the passing of time by how children grow. It's why they always say a variation of "look how tall she is getting! I remember when she was this big!" I heard that in churches as I was growing up. I remember doing it in myself in church, looking at a woman who is pregnant and then, in astonishment, at the child she had who seems to suddenly be starting school.

Our life has distinct seasons, and it can be useful to keep that in mind when making decisions.

I know, this is something older people say. I am older. We're the ones with the benefit of hindsight, even if we might be wearing rose colored glasses when we look back. But I think it's a useful frame.

When I was younger, I thought life was one long stretch of existence, an extended spring, with a vague, distant winter of old age, blurred and far away. Since my father died in his forties, I assumed I would as well, so in my imagination my future never made it past forty-six, which meant I made no practical provisions for old age.

But everything is part of a season. One season passes and is followed by another. For many, the early seasons of life are childhood, then education with its different markers; primary school, high school, for some, college. Then the beginning phase of work, or an apprenticeship or training.

For others, there are seasons within these blocks of time. My father died when I was nineteen. In the season of education/college, there was another season of grief and confusion. Illness, loss, trauma, military service, incarceration, and unemployment are all seasons as well.

The hectic, messy parental dance of hope, joy, worry and exhaustion that stretches from pregnancy or adoption through to when your youngest child starts school is a very specific season. I remember that time with joy as one of the happiest in my life. But it is tough. Unfortunately, for many families, that season runs alongside a season of increasing responsibility at work, or the accrual of new skills and challenges. Because it all costs money. For those who are saddled with student loan debt, and paying for childcare, the financial demands of this season can be acute. The physical, psychological and emotional strain of parenting young children can wear on the best of us, and cause tension for couples.

Then there is the mid-career season. For parents, it is that time when their children are in school and more independent. And the time when we're thinking about how to pay for college for our kids, fund our own retirement, and take care of our parents as they get older. We have more responsibilities but also more freedom. For those without children, it can be a time of additional responsibilities at work and a moving more deeply into our competence as we build skills and knowledge.

In our late forties and fifties, many begin another discernment process. Children may be leaving home, or starting families of their own. We often look around at that time in our lives and say I've lived many years in this kind of work, with this partner, in this place. Is it still right for me? Do I want to explore other options? Will I want to do life in this way when I am sixty? Seventy?

It might be an exterior event which closes a season. The end of a marriage. The death of a parent. A serious illness. Getting laid off. A significant financial reversal.

Ignatius says that when we are doing the Exercises, we should enjoy the literal seasons of the year. ". . . to make use of the light and pleasures of the seasons, for example, in summer of the refreshing coolness, in the winter of the sun and fire." (SE #229)

I want us to enjoy the pleasures of each season of our lives, to consider what each has to offer us, and not to rush through it in anticipation of another season. The summer does have moments of refreshing coolness, the winter does have spots of warmth and comfort. When my children were young, I was often overwhelmed, and so busy. Now that I have grandchildren, I realize what a gift it is not to rush. If my granddaughter Ruby wants to help make dinner, it takes twice as long. But we're not in a rush, we can take our time washing the carrots, and stop to line them up by size. This time I can enjoy the pleasures of the season when she's still young enough to want to sit on my lap, and run through the sprinkler in the summertime, and play with toy boats in the bathtub.

Ignatius also suggests, as we are considering how to make "a Correct and Good Choice of a Way of Life" that we consider the Third Rule: "This is to consider what procedure and norm of action I would wish to have followed in making the present choice if I were at the moment of my death. I will guide myself by this and make my decision entirely in conformity with it." (SE #186) Most of us have heard the saying that no one ever wished, on their death bed, that they had spent more time at work. Which is a nod to this Ignatian idea. What will this choice look like on my deathbed?

I find that the people who are most interested in discernment are those approaching a change of season. People in their early twenties who are considering a career choice. People in their thirties who are managing having a family while moving forward in their careers. People in their forties and fifties, often women, who are considering if they want to keep doing what they are doing for another twenty or thirty years. And anyone who is moving from one season to another because of illness or loss. The concept of a season, with its impermanence and possibilities, can be a useful frame of reference.

We'll talk more about building community in Chapter 29, but I've found great solace in having friends who are in a similar season. There are friends of the heart and friends of the road; passing temporary friendships centered around a shared activity or pursuit (of the road) as opposed to deep long-term connections (of the heart). I've always tried to find friends who are in the same season of life as I am. These low-key bonds, friends of the road, are sustaining. The kind of connection between two nurses who are in school together, or parents of school age children watching their kids compete in sports while drinking coffee and catching up, huddling under umbrellas in the rain. It's useful and reassuring to remember that most of us experience similar blessings and challenges with similar seasons or circumstances.

When my children were small and one of them was being difficult, I would say "they're just going through a stage" or "it's a phase." This was a comforting reminder that this too, would pass. That's one of the reasons I enjoy the concept of many seasons in a life. The difficult ones will pass. And our efforts and investments in one season can pay off in another season. A married couple that struggles through the early years of raising children and works hard to stay connected and together might find that early season difficult, and then reap the rewards in a later season with a deep, mature connection as an older married couple with grown children and grandchildren and the comfort of a shared history.

Sometimes we carry narratives about what a specific season is supposed to be like, and that can be either limiting or supportive. If a neurodivergent young person is told by their family that college is a joyful time where you make lifelong friends, and they, instead, experience college as hostile and overwhelming because they're not getting the support they need, they may question why their experience is so different from the narrative they've been told their whole life by a neurotypical, cis father who looks back on college as a happier time. Were the father more aware, he might recognize that his neurodivergent, gender non-conforming child could have a different experience of higher education than he did decades earlier.

In another example, a pregnant woman whose mother experienced mild postpartum depression told her daughter about the difficulties of the period after the birth of a first child. When the daughter gave birth, she felt prepared for the rigors of those first few months in a way that someone who was told that it was all sweetness and light might not be.

My narrative of a season

Because I thought I'd die young, like my father, I didn't ever plan for old age. I wanted to save for my kids to go to college, but I didn't think about my own retirement. So when, to my surprise, I was still alive in my late forties, I had to reframe my narrative about aging.

I thought about all the narratives I had heard about women aging. In my family, aging didn't seem so bad. My grandfathers were both retired when I knew them, and spent time in hobbies. One liked to garden, the other had a boat. My Italian grandmother Jenny was active in her church, community and family. She took a life changing trip to Africa as an older woman, and I still have some of the textiles she brought back. She taught me how to crochet, and made all her grandchildren blankets and was fascinated by the crafts of the places she visited. All my grandparents were active, and none of them had dementia. Both sets of grandparents owned a home and were financially comfortable. I had good examples of aging, but none that included work.

The cultural narratives around women aging are damaging and inescapable. My whole life the narrative about women aging centered on menopause. And menopause was described as an affliction. You're going to decline intellectually, physically, sexually. Aging is a somewhat shameful prospect, and its signs are best hidden behind loose clothing, artfully draped.

I really worried about this. At an ObGyn visit in my forties, I asked the doctor, a woman in her early fifties, if, indeed, the impact of menopause on my body and sexuality would be, as I had heard, like shutting off a light switch.

She smiled. "That's a story. The reality, which is proven by research, is that women like sexual variety. For many women, by the time they get to perimenopause, the years before menopause, they have been married to the same man for many years. And they're bored. The women didn't want to have sex with their husbands. But the husbands, and the male doctors, decided there was something physically wrong with the women and said it was menopause." She flipped through my chart and saw that I was, at the time, single. "Women who aren't married when they go through menopause, and have a new sexual partner or partners, see no diminishment of desire." I was so relieved. And that was my experience. Would it have been different if I had seen a male ObGyn who had told me a different, less supportive story?

Because I thought I'd die young, and I spent so many years in challenging financial circumstances, I didn't plan or save for retirement, which has consequences now. I wish I could go back to my younger self and tell her to work on her money issues sooner, to set up small automatic transfers to a retirement account. But at the time I didn't understand the concept of preparing for a later season when you're in an earlier one.

Growing up, I didn't know any older people who worked past sixty-five. But I'm still very engaged with my work. I try different things, and continue to build new skills. This is not what I expected my sixties to feel like. I don't have the financial stability my grandparents had, which means I need to continue to work. But I enjoy what I do and so that isn't an objectionable prospect. And yet, I know of few women in their sixties who still work in and around advertising and technology. I'm not saying they don't exist. There just aren't many of us still here. Which makes me feel a bit like an outlier.

Because of that, I have intentionally sought examples of women who are aging in a way I want my aging to unfold. My aunt Tanya is a lawyer who has been working for herself for years, primarily doing trusts and guardianships for people with disabilities. She says this year she's really going to retire. She's eighty. She enjoys travelling, has an active group of friends, many of them younger, and has a full life. Recently she went for a check-up and was tested for her mental competence. When she had successfully identified that the picture of the clock read ten minutes past eleven and other equally challenging content, the nurse congratulated her on her answers. "Since I'm still practicing law, I would hope I get them all right," Tanya said. She laughed when she told me that story and I thought, that's also my gene pool.

The nuns in my community are another great example of how I want to age. I'm an associate in the Congregation of St. Joseph of Peace, or CSJP. As an associate, I am part of the community and committed to further their work in the world – called a "charism" – of peace through justice. I'm a lay person, not a nun, and I don't take vows, so my role and involvement is quite different than the sisters who are vowed religious. I am one of the youngsters in the group, and these women are vitally engaged in community, social justice, and environmental issues. The work of managing the community is significant, and requires travel, long hours and hard work. Two of the current leaders are in their eighties and another is in her seventies. Seasons of service are not related to age, but to physical and mental capacity.

One of my fellow associates – men can be associates – often goes to peace protests and gets arrested. He told me how pleased he was to be arrested with a ninety-year-old nun. She was from another order, but neither of us were surprised that ninety-year-old nuns participate in social justice work to the point where they get arrested. Because the women in our community have fundamentally reframed our cultural narratives about older women.

By reconsidering the narratives I had about physical aging and working as an older person, and building community with other women who are examples of a positive way to age, I have fundamentally shifted how I approach getting older. I now believe that the next twenty years may be the most intellectually and spiritually engaging of my life.

Invitation to Explore

- What season of your life are you in? Remember, a season isn't necessarily connected to your age. How long do you think it will last?

- It might help to draw a timeline and mark out the different seasons of your life so far. Consider how each season has changed you, or what is different from season to season.

- Do you have a sense of what seasons may lie ahead for you? If your imagination, like mine did, ends earlier than your life expectancy would lead you to believe, do you know why?

- Are there investments in time you can make now that will reap rewards later in life? Think of your physical health and how often you move your body. What about relationships with your partner or spouse, children or other young people, parents, extended family, community, faith community. Who would you like to spend more time with? What is preventing you from doing that?

- Are there financial choices you can make now that will make later seasons more secure? If you, like me, struggle with saving for later years, do you know why?

- When you are in your eighties, how will you look back on the season of life you are in now? What do you think you will think then about where you are investing your time and energy now?

- Do you share relationships or community with other people who are in your same season of life? How does that support you? Does it challenge you? Would you like to add more community with people in a similar season? How might you do that? Can you think of one person who you might like to connect with to begin to form that community? While social media isn't a substitute for in person connection, it can be a good place to look for people who are in the same season you are and begin to connect there.

- Does any of this consideration of seasons give you additional thoughts around your discernment question?

Coda: An example

Some of you may be asking how these narratives connect with the question you're considering. Hopefully you have now determined what question you are asking in your discernment process, clarified your discernment map with your genuine obligations, seen what values you navigate by and reviewed various cues and promptings from your childhood and previous experience. As needed, one exercise can inform the other; for example, when you clarify your values, you may decide that your map shifts because you recommitted to a value.

In this section, you've considered narratives that limit or support you. But how do those stories influence the decision-making process? Here is an example that will show how this section on narratives ties into your discernment practice.

Let's imagine a man named Juan is making a decision about changing jobs. He is thirty-one years old.

Question: Should I take a new job in Pittsburgh working for XYZ corporation?

Obligations: My parents live in Los Angeles where I currently reside. Elderly mother with health issues. My only sibling lives in Mexico. I help my father care for my mother. I have student loans to pay off, but no other financial obligations.

Values: Prioritize family, care for the earth, relationships in community.

Cues from my past: I have always loved travel and exploration, and this job requires lots of travel. In my past two jobs, I've enjoyed being a manager and this job has a bigger team than the one I manage now. I went to college on the East Coast, but moved back to Los Angeles after graduation. I've been trying to balance my connection to home and my community here with my desire to travel and be in new places.

Narratives that Juan considered and what arose for him:

> **Work history**. I have a pattern of being Mr. Fixit – I love rescuing. At my last job I took over a department and fixed it, and that's what I'm being asked to do in this job, only on a larger scale. And I really enjoy that kind of challenge.
>
> **Money**. We had lots of financial trauma when I was younger, and it's made me reluctant to spend and worried about financial security. I need to keep that in mind because the big salary is one of the key things I like about this potential new job and the salary may take on more weight than it should for me.
>
> **Home and family**. As the youngest son, I've always been told I was the one who would stay home and take care of my parents. My father is in good health, but how long will he be able to take care of my mother without help? It would be

hard on them both if I moved away. On the other hand, I will probably need to help my parents financially in a few years and a higher paying job now could make it easier for me to help my parents if they need it later.

Spirituality. I haven't been given any kind of Divine guidance on any of this. I do believe that my uncle is a wise person who is very spiritually grounded, and he suggested that I should spend the next few years in LA since my mom doesn't have that much longer on earth and I might regret missing these last years. I feel more of a calling to be a good son than a good manager.

Rest. I know from my previous jobs that fixing a department takes a big toll on me emotionally as well as physically. It's stressful and I tend to focus just on work and ignore my health and well-being. It's clear that they regularly work long hours at this job, including all the travel. I don't know that I can have a reasonable work life balance at the Pittsburgh job. I've become accustomed to ignoring my physical well-being, but my blood pressure has crept up and my body is showing other signs of wear and tear from the stress.

Seasons. What I came up with here is that now is the time for me to take risks and explore. I don't have a partner or children, I can live and travel wherever I want. I also understand that I need to take better care of my health now if I expect to lead an active life when I am older.

As Juan adds these pieces of information, he can narrow his focus. As he considers moving to Pittsburgh to take this new job, much of what he learned by examining his narratives points to him deciding to take the job. He likes the work, it would give him more responsibility and there's lots of travel, which he enjoys. It will also be a higher salary. He's in a season of his life where he has flexibility.

But he cites that one of his key values is a responsibility to family. A bigger salary could help him support his parents financially as his mother gets frailer, but his parents would be saddened if he moved across country and his mother might not have many years left. He understands that past financial trauma can skew his perspectives about how much he really needs to earn.

Juan could decide that spending the last few years of his mother's life living near her is the best way to live out his beliefs. Or he may decide that it's best for him to build his own life away from his parents because he no longer feels that his family's narratives about his responsibilities as the youngest child work for him. His brother could participate more fully in caring for their aging parents, and there are others in their extended family who could help. Caregiving help is available, but it will mean challenging the family's expectations. Juan still hasn't made a final decision, he's just clarified and narrowed the questions that arise around his decision.

As we move into the next section, which is about different ways of deciding and specific discernment skills, Juan can build on the understanding and insights he gleaned from reviewing these stories.

Your discernment space and process will of course look much different. The idea is that we are gathering as many pieces of information as we can to inform our decision. Over time, we'll consider which pieces of information should be prioritized, and which can be considered less or disregarded.

Your Thoughts

Part Four

New Ways of Listening

When I describe the process of discernment, I say it is like solving a mystery. You are asking a question. You've clarified it and considered it with the preceding work, and that has meant carrying that question around in your awareness. It may also be in your subconscious, and leaking into dreams or daydreams or coloring your attention.

Inside of you is the answer you are seeking. But the part that knows the answer might not be able to communicate with intellect or language. It might not use reason, words, or formulas. So, it is leaving clues, like breadcrumbs, a scrap of bright cloth stuck on a bush, or the imprint of a shoe in soft earth. Your job is to find the clues. Which means you'll need to go about with your eyes open, paying attention, gathering the information you are trying to tell yourself, through these different channels, and wait.

If mindfulness is turning your awareness to the present moment, then discernment is asking your question in every present moment, and looking around for the answers. I try to look with confidence, and believe that "the right answer will come, if we want it." (BB p 69)

The following chapters will outline ways that people can receive the answers in their discernment process. First, we'll dive more deeply into the use of the imagination, especially the Ignatian Application of the Senses. Second, we'll talk about the genius of the body, how paying attention to somatic experiencing and physical sensations can guide us. Third, we'll look at the movements of attraction and aversion and how we can recognize and understand them. Finally, we'll delve into what Bill Wilson refers to as "the intuitive thought," an understanding that feels as if it comes from a deeper source.

I'd invite you to consider what kind of analogies arise for you in the next few chapters as you read about the different tools of discernment. For me, the answers to what I am discerning show up with a particular flavor. Imagine if you could taste your thoughts and emotions. You're used to a range of flavors, sweet, bitter, neutral. You might judge your thoughts and emotions by their taste. The emotions around a loss are bitter. The recollection of your time in nature, or planning for your next hiking trip may be sweet and refreshing. When I get information that is significant to my discernment process, it tastes different to me than my other thoughts, as if it comes from another source. It's similar, but weightier and more satisfying, like the difference between a stale cracker and fresh whole grain bread still warm from the oven.

Each of the approaches in this part of the book are ways to get your answers. Up to now, we've been refining the question and gathering more information. Here is where the answers begin to arrive. Listen for them.

Whatever way of listening speaks to you, the hope is that you, too will be able to become more skilled in "the discernment of spirits." My list is by no means exhaustive, and I invite you to consider any additional ways you might understand or apprehend your guidance. You may find clues in some of these, all of them, or none, but hopefully they will be a jumping off point to listen to direction from beyond your intellect.

CHAPTER TWENTY-TWO

Imagination

Imagination is one of my favorite of the Ignatian tools, and the first one I use when I am explaining this path for discernment to another person. The basic approach is this: imagine yourself in one scenario that you are considering. Ignatius is very clear that you should be using your imagination in conjunction with your senses. It's very embodied imagination.

"This will consist in applying the five senses to the matter . . . .": Ignatius begins. (SE #121). He then suggests that we "see in imagination the persons, and in contemplating and meditating in detail the circumstances in which they are and then in drawing some fruit from what has been seen." (SE #122) He then goes through hearing, smelling, tasting and touching.

Ignatius is suggesting using imagination and the Application of the Senses to put yourself into a biblical story. But the tools work for any exercise of the imagination. I suggest you consider one of the possible outcomes of the decision you are discerning. You get up in the morning and you go to your new job, for example. Look at the scene and see who is there. What does it look like, specifically? Get as detailed as you can. Listen to the sounds of nature, or imagine the conversation if there are other people present. Where are you? If you're sitting at a table, what does the table feel like? Are you eating and drinking? What do you taste? What shoes are you wearing and on what surface are you standing? Are you hot or cold? How does it feel? What does it bring up in your body, your heart, your spirit?

Someone who is discerning whether or not to leave their marriage might consider what the experience would be like to sleep alone, or to live in a space without their spouse. It might initially be difficult to move away from intellectual or emotional content attached to that idea, just as it can be challenging to quiet the mind in any meditation. Don't worry about it, just keep returning to your body. Imagine getting into bed alone. What do you hear? How do the sheets feel against your skin? You read until you are ready to sleep, you turn off the light and are alone in your bed. What is that like for you, in your body? Are your shoulders hunched? Are you cold? Or do you feel relaxed? What comes up for you under any worry or grief or anger? Is there a deeper sense of freedom and relief? Or is the deep sense more about regret and longing? Try not to anticipate your reactions or answers so you can be open to whatever might arise.

Ignatius suggests doing this exercise for hours, beginning late at night. That's not possible for many of us, but finding time where you can concentrate is a start. Usually, it's a good idea to be in a quiet place if you can. Close your eyes, if that's possible, and try to engage with your imagination as deeply as possible, imagining your embodied experience. If you are discerning a choice between two options, imagine yourself in the first option. Let's say you are considering whether to stay in the city where you live or move back home to a place where you have more family so that you can get help with childcare and more emotional support.

Consider the first option, you move back home. Imagine one aspect of that new life, perhaps what your day might be like. Slowly, without rush or judgement, imagine a scene in that day. You get up and you get the kids ready for school. What does it feel like to wake up there? What sensations do you have? What is the weather like? Imagine yourself getting in the car and driving the kids over to your mother's house so she can watch them until it's time for school. What does it feel like to carry your children's things, holding their hands, up the stairs to your mother's house? What do you hear? What does it smell like? What do you feel? Where do you feel it in your body? Sit with that for a while. Does anything arise?

Then repeat the exercise, after a rest, or at another time, and see what happens. In this case, you would consider getting up in the morning in the place you now live and dropping your kids off at the before school day care and then heading to your shift at the hospital. Note what comes up for you and see if there is any information that is useful. If not, don't worry, this is a skill that can take time to develop.

As you consider option one, you might imagine walking up to your mother's door to drop off your kids and feel a sense of peace. You may recall running up those front steps yourself and the enjoyment you had in the summers playing in the yard. But as you continue in your imagination and drive your imaginary self to your imagined work, you remember this hospital is small and understaffed. You imagine walking into the entrance and missing the excitement and challenges of the big city hospital where you work now.

Or you could have an entirely different experience. You may imagine walking up to your mother's door to drop off your kids and smelling the smoke from her cigarettes. You may have a strong sense of aversion, and not want your children to be in her house and smell like smoke when you pick them up from school later.

Intellectually, if you were making a pros and cons list, you might have put having your mother watch the kids when you have an early shift at work in the pros column – free childcare with a family member. But as you sit with that possibility in your imagination, you may realize that while that's practical, you have serious reservations about what that experience would be like for your children. Or you may realize that your current job at a big city hospital is so engaging and challenging that you don't want to leave. The hope is that you can glean additional insights, or hidden information, by using your imagination. Trying out a day or an aspect of one option in your decision-making possibilities in your imagination and understanding what emotional and intuitive information you get is one way to use your imagination. Ignatius calls it "drawing fruit" from this contemplation.

If this interests you, but you're struggling with it in practice, consider starting just with the senses. For five days, practice tuning into one sense each day. Let's say you start with sight. Pay attention to your sight throughout the day. Notice what you see. Play with sight – look at something upside down, or take off your glasses, or look through a magnifying glass. Look deeply at something in nature, a tree or a flower. Notice color. Take a walk around your neighborhood. In one block look for anything red. In the next look for anything blue – it could be a car, or a recycling bin or a discarded food container. Then yellow, green, and so on.

Try to savor the sense. When you're focusing on sound, listen to your favorite music, and maybe dance a bit. Listen to the sound of water through headphones as you go to sleep. Listen to nature sounds in real life. Take a walk and notice everything you hear. For taste, eat something that is delicious. Eat something from your youth that is evocative. For touch, go around your house and touch things with different textures, especially items that have emotional resonance, like a child's stuffed animal or the leather coat you bought with your first paycheck after college.

When you've immersed yourself in your senses for a few days, try meditating with your senses again. Just be curious. It's not a test, you don't have to do it well. Relax and see what happens. If you find fruit, rest and do this for a while. If you don't find fruit, move on.

Colloquy

Another exercise is to have a conversation in your imagination. Again, find a quiet space, or an activity that you can do in solitude. Now imagine yourself in a conversation that would be helpful. This could be the Ignatius' colloquy that I've mentioned before, where you talk to your understanding of the Divine, like Jesus, or a Saint or holy person. You might want to talk to an aspect of yourself, the artist in you, for example. It could be an ancestor or a beloved relative who has died.

Now deeply imagine yourself in conversation. What are they wearing? Where are you? What are you doing? Now ask them questions. And imagine what they would answer, how they would sound or move their hands when they talk. Pause before you imagine their answer and see if you feel inspiration.

I used to do this when I took a walk around my neighborhood. I would be talking out loud, but I figured people would imagine I was on a mobile phone with a kind of small earpiece they couldn't see. Sometimes, when I was imagining talking to the Divine, I would start crying, so I decided this was a better exercise to do alone, or in the wilderness rather than my little suburban street. I surprised myself with the strength of my reaction. But then, I have a vivid imagination and I see things clearly in my mind, like watching a movie in my head. Other people just don't have that way of imagining, and if it's not your way of imagining, there are other tools.

Art

We aren't limited to our own imaginations. Works of art can also help us in discernment. In Chapter 24 on Attraction and Aversion, I suggest paying attention to what we are drawn to or repelled by as a source of information about what we truly want, and that's especially true of art. If an older woman tells me that she has watched multiple films about a woman moving to Italy to start a new life, and she's thinking about what to do in retirement, I would draw the connection between her interest in films and stories about a woman moving to Italy and suggest she get curious about that.

Music is very evocative. You may hear songs that make you think of something related to the decision you are making. If the music on the radio or being piped through the grocery store seems to carry a message to you, don't dismiss that as adolescent foolishness. Maybe the Divine isn't playing a certain song on the radio just for you, but I do believe that once you have posed a question, parts of you will be answering that question. And we can borrow the imagination and art of others to answer that question. So, if something really gets your attention, whether it is a pop song, a hymn, Bach, or the sound of a street drummer, pay attention to it.

Visual art, dance, graphic novels, poetry, sculpture – any kind of art can inspire our imaginations and give us access to other ways of knowing. One of the first dates my husband and I went on was to the Frye Museum in Seattle. We went to an exhibit about Donald Byrd, an African American dancer and choreographer. The exhibit was small, with old videos of his early dance performances. It was interesting, but it wasn't until I saw the brochure for the exhibit that I felt that catch of breath. On the front of the brochure was a photo of Byrd as an older man, dancing on a peaked roof. One arm is up in an evocative movement, his eyes are closed, and his legs look like they are mid step. He is doing his art, as an older man, on a rooftop, and he seems so focused, so much in the right place, deeply content and grounded. I was arrested by that image. I took the brochure home and it's tucked into the edge of an old mirror in my bedroom to this day. I realized, later, that I wanted to understand how to be an artist as an older person. That image, which captured my imagination so deeply, showed me an artist, a Black man who used his art for social justice, still dancing, still using his body, apparently unfazed by being on top of a house. Maybe he loved dancing up above.

Scripture

The original way in which Ignatius used the Application of the Senses in meditation was to suggest that people doing the Exercises meditate on a scripture story. If this resonates for you, you could try this. Expand your understanding of "scripture" widely, and think of any story that speaks to you, from whatever your religious tradition or understanding deems to be Holy Word. In addition to using the Application of the Senses on the scripture story, you could also try being different people in the story. For those of us who have heard the stories in our faith tradition many times, it can break open the story and additional meanings to use our embodied imagination to place ourselves into the scene and then see what arises for us emotionally or spiritually.

I often use the Gospel story of the woman with a hemorrhage as a guided mediation to practice this technique in a retreat setting. The story (Mark 5:25-34) is about a woman who has been bleeding for a dozen years. Because she is considered to be menstruating, she is deemed unclean and is ostracized. She hasn't been able to stop the bleeding even though she spent all her money on doctors. She touches Jesus' cloak and is healed. Jesus feels power go out of himself and asks who touched him. The apostles chide him, saying they are surrounded by a jostling crowd, how can they know who touched him? But the woman comes forward and admits that she touched his cloak, and that it healed her. Jesus says her faith healed her.

As an imaginative meditation, this story is evocative for woman who have felt separated from community because of illness or patriarchal power structures. We can imagine ourselves deeply into the role of that woman, the heat of the day, the crush of people, the sensation of the blood coming out of her, the feel of the rough cloak on her fingertips, and then, miraculously being healed.

Someone else might connect to the role of the apostles, and see ways in which they themselves could be better support to the women in their lives or be open to the numinous. Yet another person may be drawn to the role of Jesus, possibly tired and overwhelmed, knowing he has power and wanting to understand more about who he is helping.

In my experience, imagining myself into a story by focusing on my senses is more evocative than studying or contemplating scripture using my intellect.

Practice

Since we're now considering the key aspects of a discernment practice, I'm going to suggest ways to practice. Up to this point, the Invitations to Explore were meant to get you thinking. The Practice suggestions at the end of the following chapters are meant to move past intellect and try other senses, approaches, and skills. If you haven't ever done a meditation practice, some of these exercises may feel odd. Try to let go of any ideas you have that there is a "right" or "wrong" way to meditate or engage with these concepts. I find it is better to do something small with regularity, than something big once in a while.

While you practice, it is important to create an environment where you can focus, as much as is feasible in your life. Turn off your phone, or computer or anything that is going to ping or beep at you or notify you of anything. Solitude is ideal, but if that's not possible try not to be around someone who will interrupt you or disturb you. Remember, Ignatius wrote spiritual *exercises*, and we may need to get used to the exercise itself for a while, like we do when we learn any other new physical skill, from cross country skiing to pickle ball. You get better the more you practice.

One

If you can make your decision into a road with two or more branches, one being yes, I do the thing the other being no, I don't do the thing, then imagine each branch, using your senses. Start with yes, I do the thing. Using your embodied imagination as described above, spend fifteen minutes in quiet contemplation of what your day would be like in that new way of living. Go through each of the senses. What arises for you? Emotions? Concerns? Insights? Then repeat the exercise with the other option, the no, I will not do the thing. See what arises for you there. Anything you want to capture for your discernment space?

Two

If your discernment question isn't binary, if it is more open, like *where should I live*, or *what kind of career do I want to pursue* you could try holding the question in your mind and imaging yourself in a completely blank space. There is no sound, no scent, nothing to see and nothing in the room except for whatever you are sitting on, if you are sitting. Now give yourself permission to fill in the space. Not with your intellect, but with a deeper wisdom. Perhaps say something to your imagination or your Higher Power or Ancestors like "go ahead, fill this in, guide me." Then see what happens. Check in with your senses. Do you smell anything? The tang of the ocean, fresh baked pie? What shows up in the room as it fills up?

Three

Is there art that inspires your imagination? It could be a song, a movie, a poem, short story or novel, architecture, a dance, any visual art. It could be a type of art or a specific piece that resonates for you.

Experience the art, intentionally. Keep part of your awareness on any cues or guidance that come up for you. Is there a particular portion of the art, or character in a story that intrigues you. Why do you think you are drawn to that? Is there information there? If you can engage with the art in an embodied way, that may deepen the experience; dancing, even seated in a chair, while listening to music; walking through a garden. One application of this might be for someone to listen to a particularly evocative piece of music every morning when they are getting ready for work and see what arises over the week.

If you are an artist yourself, consider what your art might be signaling. The first novel I ever wrote (it's unpublished) was about an alcoholic young woman. But I didn't understand she was an alcoholic until I got sober myself and looked back at the first few chapters I had written. I wrote half a book about an alcoholic, without knowing she was an alcoholic, trying to tell myself something through my own writing.

If this is fruitful, stay here for a while. Pay attention to what emotional information arises for you when you are in your imagination. It might feel like listening for an echo rather than the actual sound. Capture what arises for you, no matter how faintly.

Your Thoughts

CHAPTER TWENTY-THREE

The Genius of the Body

Once, when I was in my twenties, I walked into a room and was introduced to a man who was going to be consulting with the company where I worked. I had a strong, visceral reaction of danger. I felt it in my stomach with the force of a blow. He was a nondescript white man in his thirties wearing a suit and tie. He had a wide mouth in a truculent face. There wasn't anything that would lead me, rationally, to feel any concern. But I trusted my gut, and was wary of the man. I vaguely remember that he turned out to be a bad actor, but this isn't a story of a clear premonition. It's just the first time I remember as an adult tuning into information my body was giving me at work and listening to it.

On the other hand, the first time I met my husband I felt comfortable with him. I was nervous, yes. We were meeting for the first time at a coffee shop. But as we took a walk after having coffee, I felt grounded in my body, like my lungs had more room to expand. As we walked next to each other, I felt a physical ease and calm that I still sense, years later, every time we are together.

We often notice a physical or sexual attraction with a partner or potential lover, but there are other ways our bodies indicate connection. Openness, a sense that you can talk freely because you are understood, which may feel like a literal or metaphorical opening of your throat. You may listen differently, more attentively, or feel like you have more energy and can understand more clearly. Or there might just be a connected satisfying companionship, like mountain biking with a trusted friend.

Our bodies have a genius. By the time our intellects register that there was a noise in the house that could be dangerous, our bodies have already sent messages to our muscles and our lungs that we need to get ready. Centuries of evolution have built shortcuts where our bodies can respond before our minds get involved. But many of us have learned or been taught not to listen to our bodies. If we make decisions only using an intellectual framework, we are missing out on the intelligence our bodies can provide, as well as emotions which often show up first in the body.

If this isn't a channel we are used to listening to, how can we hear what our bodies are telling us? Think of it as tuning into a station on an old-fashioned radio with a dial. At first, the music may be far off, obscured by static, or you may hear the music clearly and then have it fade away. But keep practicing and you should be able to tune into it more reliably.

There's a reason we talk about emotions by referencing parts of our bodies; a knot in my stomach, a lump in my throat, a broken heart. Where do your emotions show up first? In your mind? In your heart? In your body? When I am upset, my stomach clenches like a fist, and my breathing becomes shallow. When I am happy, my muscles feel looser, and my breathing is easy and open.

To really listen to our internal wisdom, we need to be able to tune into our bodies. For some of you, that will be easy, your body is comfortable, familiar territory. But for many of us, that might be challenging. (See Chapter 27 for specifics for dealing with trauma, physical disabilities or other ways in which life experience can make being present in your body especially difficult.)

Here are examples of ways of listening to your body. In keeping with the Jesuit suggestion to "rest where you find fruit" if one or more of these don't resonate, then skip them. My hope is that you can find one or two ways to connect with your body that you can practice.

You probably already know how to do this

It may be useful to consider times where you received information and felt connected to your body in your past, so you can frame this as a return to an innate ability, rather than a new skill to learn. Step Two in the Twelve Steps says, "Came to believe that a Power greater than ourselves could restore us to sanity." (BB P. 59) First, we *came to believe*. It's a process, it takes time. Second, *could restore*; it is possible to be restored to something we had once, but lost. We can reconnect to a conduit between body and mind that was blocked or impeded but can be reestablished. That's how I think of this, we are being restored to a connection with our bodies that may have been lost or obscured.

Can you think of any times in the past where you received a strong signal from your body? Think especially of childhood. It might have been a signal of basic needs, like hunger or thirst, heat or cold. Or it might have been a strong emotion, like love, fear, excitement, or sorrow. Can you remember a time in the past when your body gave you information? Does that help you reframe this as an innate ability that might have become obscured?

Can you think of a time of deep connection or comfort that you experienced physically when you were younger? It could be with another person, it could be alone, in nature, or with a pet or other animal. Take a moment to return to that time. Close your eyes and take a deep breath. Without going into your mind, telling yourself a story, or having any judgement, just remember what happened. Where did you feel the emotion or sensation in your body? There's no right or wrong answer, and if you can't focus on any specific sensations that's ok too.

Have you ever had an experience like I did, where you were given a warning from your body about a person, situation or place? What was that like? Where did that sensation show up in your body? Did you listen to it or ignore it?

Conversely, can you think of a time when your body said yes, this is a good place, or a positive person or situation? I often write at a space in Bellevue, Washington. I'm sitting here right now. It's by Lake Washington, and I can look through the evergreens and see the water from where I sit. A bald eagle just flew over the trees, wheeling slowly. Every time I park my car in the upper lot and walk down the long stairway, my spirit lifts as soon as I see the water. This place feels welcoming and restful to me, and my body reacts positively, like oh yay! Every time.

If your youth doesn't give you information about ways in which you listened closely or were guided by your body, you could try to think of activities that make you feel connected to your body as an adult. When do you feel especially tuned into your body? If you were or are active, can you think of physical sensations around activity that made you aware of your body? We live near Puget Sound and the shock of the cold water as I dive in is frightening and exhilarating. There is a sense of mystery – what kind of animals are in the water below me? Swimming in a beautiful natural setting makes me feel adventurous and brave, I relish the sensations of my arms and legs moving easily through the water.

Perhaps food and drink open the conduit between your awareness and your body. A good meal with friends, a glass of wine, cookies warm from the oven, the sensations of kneading yeasted dough on a floured board, that favorite carryout meal or coffee drink.

If you have a meditation or prayer practice, does your body chime in? Many people experience physical sensations while they are meditating. Sometimes it is discomfort or pain. When I first started meditation, I would sometimes shake. It was soon after I got sober, I was living in a little apartment in East Palo Alto in Northern California, and I would meditate on the couch after the kids went to sleep. We had earthquakes, and at first, I thought we were having a small earthquake, because I felt a slight shaking. But it seemed unlikely that we had earthquakes at the same time every night when I was meditating. I realized the slight thrumming sensation I thought was the earth moving was my legs shaking. I found out that other people experience this. The Quakers are called Quakers because they used to shake during services. The actual name of the organization is the Society of Friends. I was doing a small quake. Sometimes when I pray, I cry, out of nowhere. Does anything come up for you in prayer, meditation, or any meditative practice? I use meditative practice broadly – it could be hiking in the woods, surfing, gardening.

Sexuality can be a great way to connect to your body, and tune into the messages it can give you. Can you think of sensual experiences, alone or with another person, where another emotion arose; it might be light or dark. Have you ever cried or laughed after sex, not from sadness or humor or in reaction to something happening in the here and now, but as another channel opening up?

Focusing on the specific senses as I mentioned in the previous chapter can also unblock channels here, since the body is also the seat of our senses. Try experiences that engage your senses, like deeply inhaling the fragrance of hot chocolate and then tasting it and savoring it.

You could also use your body in a different way than you customarily do. As adults, we don't often move our bodies in experimental or playful ways. If you are able, you could try a cartwheel or lie down on the grass in the sun or make a snow angel on your back, moving your arms up and down in the snow. It could be yoga on a beach or just stretching your arms up above your head in the morning. I like to swim laps, which is very adult, and at the end of my lap swimming I'll do a few somersaults in the water. Just to be upside down for a minute, to play. I did this last week and a young man leaving the pool looked twice, then gave me a thumbs up. Maybe I gave him a new narrative about aging.

Once you have remembered how you can get information or emotions from your body, once you ground yourself in the knowledge that this is a skill you already have, you can figure out ways to practice this so you can use it as a part of your discernment process.

Practice

First, choose a way in which you are going to listen to your body this week. It may be one of the examples listed above, or it may be your own. Pick a time or place where you are going to practice. Try to do it every day, if possible, or least three times in the week if you can. A short session often is better than a long session occasionally.

As you start the practice, first, return to the question you are discerning. What is it that you want to know? Then ask your body. It might feel weird, but try asking your body for guidance. Then listen. You'll need to do this over time, and be patient. This comes easily to some people and for others it is more difficult. For those who are challenged by this path, don't worry, there are other paths available that might be more useful for you.

Try the activity or put yourself in the circumstance where you are most connected to your body. Let's imagine it's taking a walk in nature. Ask your body the question you are considering and ask for guidance. Walk. Try to be in a contemplative frame. When thoughts arise, any thought, just let it go. I imagine my thoughts floating downstream, and I'll picture myself on the shore, watching the thought go by. I don't need to wade out and get on the thought-raft. I don't need to engage with the thought at all, I can just watch it float by.

Try noticing your senses, again, without thought or judgement. We're not imagining what our senses would be experiencing as we were in the last chapter; we are tuning into our senses and what they are literally sensing at this moment to ground us in our body. What do you smell? How does the path feel on your feet? Are you warm, cold? If you drink water, what does it taste like, is it cold? How does it feel going down your throat? What do you see? Notice the path, the grass, the trees, individual leaves and weeds. What do you hear? Try doing a body scan – start at the top of your head and just consider your body, through your face and jaw, your shoulders, arms and hands, down through your trunk, your legs and feet. Where do you experience areas of tension? Where do you feel strong?

If sensations arise, resist the urge to tell yourself a story about the sensation. Instead of telling yourself that you're angry because your boss is such a jerk try saying "I'm feeling tension in my shoulders, and I feel emotionally activated in a way that that signals anger to me. I'm going to just walk with this a while, and see what else comes up."

This morning, I woke up with a pain in my shoulder. I didn't strain it. I wasn't exercising in any way that would hurt my shoulder. As I leaned against the wall with a tennis ball between wall and shoulder to massage the painful place, I traced the outlines of the aggrieved muscle, an angry knot. I was stretching and considering scheduling a massage as a practical response, while also being curious about what my body might be telling me with this pain. It felt cranky, overburdened, ambushed. I didn't know what that was about, but I sat with it, considering, being aware.

For me, I think of it as being in a dialogue with my body. Really paying attention, being open and interested in what my body has to say, with the same attention I would offer a person I love, or a pet. If your young, active dog suddenly began to limp, you would be attentive, curious, perhaps even concerned. You'd take her paw and try to find the source of her discomfort. Try to do the same thing with your body as you do this practice.

Then wait. See what comes up. Continue listening. Information and emotions might not arise while you are walking, it might happen when you are driving home from the walk, or cutting up tomatoes for dinner. Often my body only gives me information later, after I engage with it. I've cried in many gym showers after swimming, for example, because that's a place where my body has lots to tell me – not during the activity, but after.

Keep listening. If you try one path, like walking in nature, and you don't get much there, then try another path, maybe dancing. Keep listening. Write down what arises for you and put it in your space.

Your Thoughts

CHAPTER TWENTY-FOUR

Attraction and Aversion

One of the ways in which we give ourselves clues is through attraction and aversion. What calls to us, attracts us, engages our attention? What repels us? This way of listening doesn't need to include the body, so it may be useful for people who aren't drawn to body genius. Attraction and aversion can be based in the body, but it can also be a more aesthetic or emotional path.

Our culture celebrates attraction. What we are drawn to, what calls us, what compels us. Often, we give short shrift to what we dislike as a potential guide. Focusing on the negative is dismissed as, well, too negative. I'm inviting you to reframe that narrative.

In theology, there is something called "apophatic" understanding. I'm going to sidestep the theological complexity of this phrase, and use it simply for our purposes here. Apophatic belief means knowing the Divine by identifying what the Divine is not. That is a valid way to understand the Divine. A person may say that they can't believe in a God who smites, who is vengeful, or who excludes people who are hurt, weak or alone. They have faith in God, it is real faith, they know that their Higher Power would never do certain things. They just may not be able to say what their Higher Power would do. But that faith is as valid as the faith of someone who can cite dogma and doctrine. In fact, the apophatic path can signal a greater spiritual maturity precisely because it doesn't have easy answers or lots of cultural support, and it requires more labor than a belief system someone else built that a person never challenges or questions.

Apophatic also means emptying out. Empty of words, of belief, of dogma, of content. So often, people who are struggling to understand their concept of the Divine feel a cultural pressure to say what God is for them, to align with a specific faith tradition, to adopt a path to God that is full of words and images. This is called the "kataphatic" approach. Ignatian theology is kataphatic. It is as full of words and images as a fruitcake. Centering prayer and other mantra based meditative practices are apophatic.[1] And an apophatic path or process is equally valuable.

In contrast to the fruitcake of Ignatian theology, I want us to consider the spacious emptiness of apophatic awareness as a useful counterpoint. Knowing you don't want to do something is valuable. Believing clearly in what the Divine is not can be a strong foundation upon which to build a vital faith. Being repulsed by something that is not, on its face, negative or repulsive can be a way your spirit is communicating with you. Since it doesn't have many words, aversion or apophatic awareness isn't often described – how do you describe empty? How do you demonstrate the value of zero? Because there aren't words for it, lots of people aren't taught how to listen to or value the empty, the negative, the "not this."

Here's an example of how attraction and aversion can show up. A woman and her partner are deciding whether to have a child. Her male partner has always wanted children and has made it clear that he wants a long-term relationship that includes children. The woman, let's call her Lisa, has never really wanted children, but also isn't opposed to the idea. She loves her partner, and is in the process of discerning if she wants children with him. The stakes are high, since if she decides she doesn't want children, she believes the relationship will end. Because of that, it's been hard to "hear" any internal guidance. She keeps popping into her rational mind or feeling overwhelmed emotionally with the thought of her relationship ending. Lisa tries an intentional decision-making process of discernment. Lisa goes to visit her older sister, who recently had her second child. Because Lisa is in her discernment process, she shows up for this visit open to what the experience might tell her.

If Lisa were to have an attraction response, she might discover a strong physical enjoyment in the baby. The newborn baby smell, the connection she feels with her infant nephew as he snuggles into her neck. When he falls asleep on her chest, she feels a deep peace and comfort and almost drifts off herself. She sees that her sister is tired, and that her niece, who is three years older, is having a bit of trouble adjusting to the new baby. She clearly recognizes that there are challenges in this season of her sister's life, but the rhythm of it seems appealing, the gently tyranny of raising two young children.

Her sister talks about her recovery from a difficult birth and Lisa thinks about what a powerful experience it must be to bring a new life into the world. When

1 https://www.ignatianspirituality.com/kataphatic-or-apophatic-prayer/

her sister is nursing the baby, Lisa goes into the kitchen to do the dishes. As she cleans up and rinses out bottles, she imagines doing this for her own child. She thinks about having a child with her partner and the connection that would be for them. What would it be like to make another person together? She is curious about what their baby might look like – would it have her partner's curly hair or her straight hair? She feels a calm, pleased anticipation. Lisa doesn't want to leave; she enjoys being in the middle of all the bustle. She helps get her niece ready for bed, reading her a bedtime story on her niece's new big girl bed.

If Lisa were to have an aversion response, she might find that she is put off by things she notices as if for the first time, although she was around when her niece was a newborn. As she walks into the apartment and is greeted by her niece, Lisa suddenly notices how everything smells and she feels a visceral sense of distaste. She hides it from her sister, and manages her expression, but her niece has that scent of sweaty toddler, and hasn't had a bath in days. The baby's diaper needs to be changed and the whole room smells like baby poop and her sister's slightly rancid body odor. When she holds her nephew, she feels uncomfortable, a combination of worry and dread. He's so small, she thinks she would be terrified to be responsible for a human being who was that tiny. What if she drops him? When her sister talks about her recovery from a difficult birth, Lisa is horrified. She tries to imagine being cut open to take a child out in a C Section, the incision, the pain, the insult to her body. When her sister nurses the baby Lisa realizes she has always been uncomfortable about the thought of nursing an infant herself. She doesn't think she could ever think of her breasts as anything but milk producers after that experience. She helps her sister with chores around the house, but can't wait to leave. When she gets home, she puts on her running shoes and takes a long run, feeling an intense sense of relief that she is away from her sister's home and children, that her body is still her own, she can run and be strong and whole. Because she understands the power of an aversion reaction, she doesn't judge herself for it, or categorize her thoughts or emotions as "bad" or "judgmental." It's all information, and it's coming from a deep true part of herself. She loves her sister and her niece and nephew; she just recognizes that she has clear information from her aversion that this is not what she wants to be doing at this time in her life.

Of course, our movements of attraction or aversion might not be that dramatic or obvious. But the more we listen to where our inclinations lie, the better we'll get at finding and following these particular clues, especially if we can do so without judgement of ourselves. Welcome the negative, the aversion, the no.

What gets in the way?

Sometimes it's hard to tune into this channel. For many of us, what we like and dislike hasn't been honored, or it's been denied or shamed. Think of something like a sexual attraction to someone of the same gender. In parts of the world, acting on that attraction can lead to rejection, shame and even physical danger. Just having the thought is condemned by certain faith traditions.

How many things that we don't like are we told we have to do anyway? When I was growing up, children had to go over and kiss the disgusting family friend or get a hug from the aunt with the sharp nails and chin whiskers that hurt your face. The fact that we didn't want to be hugged or kissed or have our hair mussed or have to answer fatuous questions about if we had a boyfriend, at age seven, didn't play into the equation. What did that teach us about the validity of our aversion? "Be nice to Aunt Sally, don't be rude to Uncle Victor." Being nice meant stifling your aversion, your agency over your body, while honoring it was "rude" and could be punished.

For people who have been shamed and judged about the size of their bodies, what does it mean when our natural, innate attraction to food is judged and shamed? People will look askance at a larger person eating a dessert in public but acclaim with admiration when they see a slim person eat the same dessert – how do you do it? How many times have we been told what kind of food is "good" and what is "bad" with no reference to what our bodies really want? Food is a place where, for many of us, our attractions or aversions are so dismissed or overridden that we can lose track of what we actually enjoy. The idea of eating for enjoyment, for sensual pleasure, can be completely lost.

In his book *The Screwtape Letters*, C.S. Lewis suggests that loving a specific, odd thing, in spite of social pressure not to, can keep us closer to the Divine. He talks about a man who really loves tripe. Holding onto our idiosyncratic attractions, even when and if others mock us, strengthens us to hold on to other values or goals; Lewis suggests it can make us more spiritual. "I have known a human defended from strong temptations to social ambition by a still stronger taste for tripe and onions."[3]

I think the value is in us owning our own specificity, and respecting and honoring ourselves by, where possible, moving towards what attracts us and away from what repels us. But even noticing and naming what repels or draws us can yield important information in our discernment process.

[3] C.S. Lewis, *The Screwtape Letters*, HarperCollins e-books, Chapter 13, p. 66 3

Temptation

We can also be misled by attraction and aversion. I know the word "temptation" carries lots of baggage in various religious traditions, but it's the most useful word here. Sometimes we are attracted to experiences, actions or people that go against our value systems or beliefs. At other times we are strongly resistant to actions that are in line with our value systems.

Temptation is the desire to follow the pull of attraction or aversion even when it moves us away from our beliefs, promises or commitments. Alcoholics know about temptation. I remember staring at the label on a bottle of Southern Comfort. I didn't even like Southern Comfort when I was drinking. But when they started selling liquor at grocery stores, I found myself, sober, mesmerized by the label on a bottle of Southern Comfort. *Look, I thought, there's a picture of a lady in a skirt walking up to a door. How inviting. I should buy that.*

Once I was on a flight in January 2000. *I can drink on a plane, right? I mean, we're in the sky, does it count? Besides, it's been so many years since I drank that all the cells in my body are different. It's a new millennium! Surely, I can drink now.*

I didn't drink in either of those cases, but I felt like I understood the Siren Song metaphor better. In Homer's Odyssey, Odysseus ties himself to the mast so he doesn't hurl himself into the sea because the songs of the Siren are so compelling. He tells his companions, whose ears are plugged with beeswax so they can't hear the songs, not to release him no matter how much he begs. He hears the song. He begs to be freed. His friends refuse and the boat moves away from the Sirens and Odysseus is safe.

"There are cases where our ancient enemy, rationalization, has stepped in and has justified conduct which was really wrong, the temptation here is to imagine we had good motives and reasons when we really didn't." (12X12 p. 94)

I can tell the difference between temptation and attraction or temptation and aversion by the noise in my head. When I am tempted to do or not do a thing, there's a lot of chatter in my internal community. *I deserve this thing. My adherence to this ethical standard is outmoded, out of touch, hopelessly old fashioned.* I will come up with complex and convoluted arguments as to why the thing I know is not right might be right if I just look at it at a different angle. If there's a brass band of justification and rationalization in my head, I know that this is probably temptation and not authentic attraction or aversion.

Genuine attraction and aversion are quieter. They show up for me with a strong, almost incontrovertible command. This is something I want. Or I don't want. No brass band, no big intellectual arguments. I often feel it more in my body or emotions.

If you're not sure, it is useful to have a friend or trusted advisor to run this by so you can confirm that you're not being bamboozled by temptation masquerading as a spiritual signpost. But it isn't something you can decide by canvassing your friends and family – what they might do isn't always what's best for you.

As I've mentioned, I was estranged from my mother for most of the last two decades of her life. Making the decision to be estranged from a parent is never easy, and most of us who have done it have good reasons. I had good reasons. People who discovered this about me always had lots of opinions. I should be more spiritual so I could forgive my mother. I should have more compassion. It would change when she was dying. Would I see her on her deathbed? People often asked that question; they were obsessed with this deathbed conversation, years before she had any health issues. "You'll regret it for the rest of your life if you don't see her on her deathbed," women would tell me, women who had good relationships with their mothers, or who had come into better relationships as they aged.

I did have compassion for my mother. But it wasn't emotionally safe for me to be around her, so I wasn't. The aversion that I had to my mother was physical. If she touched me, my flesh shrank away, I recoiled and felt sick to my stomach. My decisions around how I participated in my mother's last months of life were intentionally made. I honored my aversion and didn't see her. Plenty of people didn't approve. I did see her once as she was dying, briefly. It wasn't healing or helpful to me, and I don't know if it helped her. She died later that night. I did it because it was important to my Aunt Tanya, my mother's sister who was caring for her. The desire to help my aunt was more important than my aversion.

This was a situation where my aversion was spiritual direction. I didn't have a lot of noise in my head about it. The advisors I trusted supported me in my course of action, even though many people would have criticized or judged my choices. At the end the aversion turned into a temptation not to do something I believed was right – honoring my aunt's wish that I would see my mother on her deathbed. So, I went.

Your value system, your ethical framework, can and should be congruent with the direction you are getting from aversion and attraction. If it isn't, then sit with it. It took me a long time to understand that the commandment to honor my father and mother didn't mean that I had to give an abusive parent unrestricted access to me, that it was important to listen to the intense aversion that arose when I was near her.

Practice

Consider what attracts you and what repels you. What does aversion mean to you? Do you think that aversion is less skillful, a withdrawal from a sensation that should be pushed through or welcomed? Can you reclaim aversion as a useful guide? Maybe do some writing or have conversations about how to honor what you feel pushed away from in a way that is valid and affirming.

Notice, over the span of a week or two, where you feel either attraction or aversion. Where possible, try to honor those movements within you. If you find that difficult, put yourself in a situation where you can do something that attracts you. It doesn't matter what it is, as long as you genuinely are drawn to it in a way that comes from you. Think of the idiosyncratic things you love. It could be a swim in a lake, a zombie movie or the *lengua* tacos. Enjoy the thing you are attracted to and see what comes up for you, if anything.

If you like writing things down, if you're a natural journal writer or list keeper, try tracking your aversion or attraction for a week. Jot it down – what you felt, where and when. If nothing else, it can be good practice in noticing those movements in yourself.

Have you ever had an experience where attraction and aversion were actually temptation in disguise? How did you know the difference? Have you seen that in someone else's life choices? We're here to identify and name, not to judge, to understand what temptation looks like, sounds like and feels like for us or others.

Does the attraction or aversion you are experiencing give you any information about the question you are discerning? Are you getting guidance, however diffuse or vague that guidance may seem at first? What is it telling you?

Your Thoughts

CHAPTER TWENTY-FIVE

The Intuitive Thought

My daughter and son-in-law don't go to church, but they like it that I take my granddaughter to church. So, when I talk to Ruby about spiritual matters, I try to be respectful of the fact that her parents' beliefs differ from mine.

"What are these?" she asked, pointing to a drawing in the church bulletin of three angels, wings extended.

"Those are angels."

"What are angels?"

"Well, some people believe . . ."

It's what I'm trying to do here, be inclusive. "Some people believe . . ." "Many have experienced . . ." Phrases like these are meant to invite us to develop our own understanding of the Divine, whatever that may be, even if your belief is that there is no God.

A few weeks ago, I was trying to explain prayer to Ruby. Which meant explaining more about God. And prayer as talking to God. Who you can't see. Ruby, at four, was curious about a God she couldn't see. I told her some people could feel God.

"I don't feel God," she said, with finality.

"Well, maybe you need to practice. I can feel God."

"Nope, I don't feel God."

"That's fine."

Later, when I thought about it, I wondered. What if she doesn't feel God because God is all around her? Do fish feel water? When she brought it up again, and asked me to tell her more about the feel God thing, I suggested that. "Maybe you do feel God, but you're so surrounded by God that that is all you know."

She considered this. We were driving back from church. She was in her car seat in the back, and I could see her little face get serious as she thought about it.

"Can we listen to Dora the Explorer?" she said.

Theology lesson over.

I wanted to have a chapter for people who feel the Divine or a Higher Power. I don't want to exclude those who don't – you may be so surrounded as to never have a sense of apartness. I'd like to welcome those who feel the Divine, even sporadically, with specific guidance.

The Intuitive Thought

People in Twelve Step programs will sometimes refer to "an intuitive thought." It comes from the chapter, *Into Action,* when explaining how to start one's day.

> *"In thinking about our day, we may face indecision. We may not be able to determine which course to take. Here we ask God for inspiration, an intuitive thought or decision. We relax and take it easy. We don't struggle. We are often surprised how the right answers come after we have tried this a while. What used to be the hunch, or the occasional inspiration gradually becomes a working part of the mind. Being still inexperienced and having just made conscious contact with God, it is not probably that we are going to be inspired at all times. We might pay for this presumption in all sorts of absurd actions and ideas. Nevertheless, we find that our thinking will, as time passes, be more and more on the plane of inspiration. We come to rely on it." (BB p. 86-86)*

We're here, together, because you are facing indecision. You don't know what course to take. If you have a spiritual practice that includes asking a Higher Power for guidance, this is the time and place to do that.

Here we ask God for guidance, an intuitive thought or a decision.

Ask. If you're not used to praying, try talking out loud to your Higher Power as you would to a person. We're returning here to the Ignatian suggestion about a colloquy, a conversation with the Divine. It may feel awkward, it may feel good. It doesn't matter how it feels, it can be effective regardless. Ask your Higher Power your question. Ask for guidance in making the decision. I often ask God not to be subtle because I won't get it, I need the loud version. You can do this while you're driving to work, or you can place yourself by a mountain stream. You can light a candle or go to a place of worship, or you can do it as you're drifting off to sleep. Imagine that your Higher Power is very interested in what you have to say, as interested as you are in hearing the thoughts of someone you love dearly. Imagine that you are the Beloved of God.

Does your understanding of the Divine need to evolve? Many spiritual cultures act as if an understanding of the Divine is static. You find God, or someone gives you a conception of God, and that's your understanding of God for the rest of your life. Done and dusted. What I like about the Higher Power concept is that you can change your Higher Power at any time, all by yourself, with no other authority than your own understanding. Implicit in the Higher Power idea is an understanding that your conception will evolve as your spiritual maturity increases.

This can be hard to swallow for people who grew up in a faith tradition that had very specific ideas about who God was. Male, stern, white beard, smiting, angry. You can't just make up a God. Them's smiting words. But once you get over that, there's a freedom in the idea.

I'm going to repeat an exercise from Chapter 19, Spirituality. Take a piece of paper and draw a line down the center. On the left side of the paper write down everything you were told about who the Divine is. On the right side, write down what you would like your Higher Power to be like. If there was something good in your old conception on the left, you can add it on the right. See what comes up for you.

My understanding of the Divine continues to evolve. I'm a very visual person, so I've prayed to a God who was a woman. I had a very detailed understanding of what she looked like – she was big, and strong. There've been times, like when I was doing the Spiritual Exercises, that I thought of Jesus in that role, and focused on what Jesus was like as a man. The older I get, the wider my understanding of the Divine is, I am more prone to use the word Divine than God, since God is so often associated with the old school smiting white beard guy.

An old friend from work is Hindu, and in his apartment he had a statue of Ganesh. He explained his devotion to Ganesh, and I was enchanted. I want to invite you to borrow any aspect of the Divine from any tradition that resonates with you. Of course, we should be mindful of appropriating the religious traditions, symbols or practices of other groups, especially when those groups have been oppressed or marginalized like Indigenous peoples. But in private, respectfully, nurture anything that connects you to the Divine.

Different saints have spoken to me at different times. Not as deity, but as guide. I'm a big fan of Teresa of Avila, who was powerful, had a bad temper, argued with God, and changed the Catholic Church. I have my grandmother Frances' devotion to St. Joseph, a comforting devotion for fatherless women. Saints can be useful interlocutors, and it can be heartwarming to see how often they failed in their lives. They wanted to be good, but just couldn't quite manage it consistently.

For some it is their ancestors that they honor and turn to for guidance. My father's mother, christened Zenia, had her name changed to Jenny when she came to Ellis Island from Italy. She was killed in a car crash when I was in my twenties. A few years ago, my aunts gave me textiles she brought back from a trip she took to Africa. She took the trip with a woman friend and described it as a life changing experience. I have the textiles that she brought in my study, draped over the trunk next to the antique drafting table where I write. That's an altar, a way of honoring my grandmother.

In whatever way you approach the Divine or any interceding entities is good. Stay with it and then wait.

We relax and take it easy. We don't struggle.

Keep waiting. Wait and believe you'll get guidance. Even if you don't believe, pretend that you do. Keep asking. You can pray every day, or maybe you set up a small intention altar in your home with a candle or smooth stones that remind you that you're waiting. And wait. Don't struggle. Stay alert and open to ways in which the Divine may show up.

We are often surprised how the right answers will come.

Years ago, Mary Virginia, my oldest friend, and I were talking about how we could get guidance from God. We thought maybe we couldn't, that it wasn't that direct. We both grew up Catholic, but struggled with the concept of a personal God, one who might intervene directly in our lives by giving us direction.

"It's not like God's going to send down turtledoves, or have the angel Gabriel show up on our doorstep," she said. We laughed knowingly, silly us, thinking that God was going to send us messages.

The next day she called me. She sounded a little surprised. She told me that when she woke up and went downstairs there were two doves sitting on a telephone wire outside her kitchen. She lives in Eastern Washington, she'd never seen doves at her house before.

Then later that day, there was a knock at her door. She pulled the door open and saw a stranger, a good-looking man, tall with blonde curls. He said "Hi, I'm Gabriel." He was an old law school buddy of her husband's. She'd never seen him before, he's the only person either one of us have ever known who goes by the full name Gabriel.

We had a reaction I think many of us have – wanting to believe, but then thinking, nah. That can't be true. But what if it is?

I've had, at this point in my life, many intuitive thoughts. For me it feels like a thought with a glow, like highlighter over a phrase in a book. It comes into my head as a new idea or understanding, not arising from an association or other thoughts. It is more like a stone dropped into my awareness. It's there. It has a light, scent or sound that is different than other thoughts. I know the difference now, and when I sense an intuitive thought, I pay attention.

I remember the first time this ever happened to me. I was newly sober and getting a divorce from my children's father. I didn't want to get divorced, he did. I thought divorce was a failure, because the Catholic Church, and my family, said it was a failure. I didn't pray about it, because I thought I already knew what God would say – no, don't get divorced. I was walking down a street in California on a warm afternoon, and I tried asking God for guidance. Should I get divorced? I had this swift intuitive thought: leave him. It is the best thing for you and the children. Give him the divorce. Let it go.

The authority of this concept was that it was diametrically opposed to what I expected. My idea of God would never have said that. When I heard it, when I experienced the depth and weight of it in my body, I asked myself what if *this* is God and I was wrong before? It was loud. Like a piercing whistle in a noisy crowd, it got my attention. Still, it took me a while to understand that this was what I should do, it was the best thing for me and the children. And I did it. It was the right decision.

Can you think of a time when you had something like the intuitive thought I'm describing? It could have been something about yourself, or another person, guidance or a new awareness or understanding. It might come from our subconscious, our higher self, a collective unconscious, our Ancestors or God. But to me it's real, and if you can feel that, or learn how to feel that, then it can be a vital part of your discernment process.

You will probably have to practice. You will have to *try this for a while.* You may already know how to do this, if you have or had a spiritual practice or a way of being connected to nature that facilitated this inner knowing at another time in your life. You can try reconnecting to that.

The religious scholar Karen Armstrong often suggests that there are people who have a talent for spirituality. If you live in a secular community and don't have a faith tradition, you might not know you have a talent for spirituality. There are religions that downplay direct connection with God, or mystical experiences. In the Catholic tradition I grew up in mystics were old saints long dead, not anyone who lived now. But people with the talent for spirituality exist, just like people who can do complicated math in their heads or have perfect pitch. We might have that talent and don't know it because we aren't in a community or culture that values spirituality.

Many of us have a longing for a spiritual connection. Spiritual writers have described it as being homesick for God. Our capitalist culture tries to convince us that what we long for is greater success or wealth, or that we want the love of a person, or that we can achieve belonging by buying this or that. C.S. Lewis first experienced his longing for God as a fascination with Norse mythology. A longing can be expressed initially in a taste for the fantastic, the numinous, but we might be told that we are childish, or just deluded. Many have noticed that another word for alcohol is spirits, and suggested that alcoholics crave a spiritual connection and mistake spirits for spirituality as they try to fill a "God shaped hole" with substances.

St. Augustine in his *Confessions* writes "You have made us for yourself, O Lord, and our heart is restless until it rests in you." I've felt that restlessness and looked for something here, tangible, that will alleviate it. If you relate to the idea of being homesick for God, or having a spiritual restlessness, you might have a talent for spiritualty. The very fact that you are reading this might indicate a longing, a curiosity, a drawing towards.

> *Being still inexperienced and having just made conscious contact with God, it is not probable that we are going to be inspired at all times. We might pay for this presumption in all sorts of absurd actions and ideas.*

I do want to acknowledge that there are risks when we first start learning about intuitive thoughts or guidance. That's why it is useful to have someone to run your intuitive thoughts by. In the Ignatian tradition this is a spiritual director. In Twelve Step work it is a sponsor.

So, if you get an intuitive thought that you should sell all your belongings and move to another country, you may be right. But find someone you respect and tell them about your plan. Because you might also be wrong. If it's from God, it'll get stronger. If it's not from God, it'll probably seem less urgent over time.

> *Nevertheless, we will find that our thinking will, as time passes, be more and more on the plane of inspiration. We come to rely upon it.*

This takes time, practice, exercise. It might be days, weeks, months or years. If we have other spiritual practices that are geared toward service and working for the good of others or the earth, that will fuel the process of connecting to intuitive thoughts. I heard a sermon once, given by a Jesuit priest, who said if you want to find God, help others. Don't worry about finding God, just help others and God will show up.

Practice

Is there a spiritual practice you could do every day for two weeks? It could be any of the explorations offered so far in this book, or it could be reading from a spiritual text or a period of daily prayer or mediation. It is better to do three minutes every day than it is to do a longer period once a week. This is practice, which means some days will be fruitful and others won't.

Pick a time or circumstance in which to do your chosen spiritual practice. I am more likely to remember to pray if I associate the prayer with another task. There is a set of prayers I say every morning in the shower, because I take a shower every morning. In fact, I'm so in the habit that if I get in the shower at the gym later in the day, I automatically start the prayers. I meditate after breakfast but before work. Every day. I have meditated with a large dog on my lap, and later, a quiet toddler. Animals and children seem to be drawn to meditation. Some days I feel connected, other days my head is full of noise and I realize, again, that I am not good at meditation. Which doesn't matter. I still get the benefits. When I worked a job where I drove into Seattle every day, I would pray on the drive there and on the way home I would do the Examen, a Jesuit process of self-examination. The point is, you can have spiritual practice, prayer and meditation in the midst of your daily life, no matter how crowded it may be.

Begin your session of spiritual practice by centering your discernment question. Try asking your Higher Power to give you guidance. Then do whatever your practice is.

You might not get answers right away. Consider your expectations about your spiritual practice. I had this idea that I'd feel super connected and get guidance while I meditated. But sometimes very little happens during my meditation or prayer. I often don't feel holy or connected or anything but distracted. Often the intuitive thought or insight happens later in the day, or the following day. Use all the tools we have discussed so far to keep listening; tune into your body, your attraction and aversion responses, art, dreams, whatever resonates with you. Write down what comes up for you in the space you are using for your discernment work.

Where are we now?

At this point, you have completed the main elements of the discernment practice. Next, we're going to discuss navigating potential blockages and building a support system for sustaining this process. But first, let's check in on the process up to this point, if you are doing it linearly, which you may not be.

I'd invite you to return to the space you have been using to record your work so far. Has anything changed? Are there concepts or ideas that have evolved? Do you have new guideposts or information?

Do you have enough information to decide? Do you have an answer? I'm not always sure when I have an answer. If you do have a guide, this would be a good time to check in. Or you can sit with the answer you think you have. Try it on the way you might test drive a car or wear a new coat or shoes for a few days. While it might be unfamiliar at first, does it feel right over time?

You might be done. You might have had your answer at any point in this process, or you might be diligently applying yourself and find that the answer eludes you for months. Again, this isn't a school assignment, there won't be a grade. Your process is unique to you, and there is no reason to rush it or judge it.

If you don't have any answers, if you feel frustrated that you've been participating in this process throughout and getting nothing but static on all the channels you try, don't be discouraged. You're still developing the skills, building new neural networks, and coordinating tiny muscles that can one day all fire together and surprise you. You may be in a season of desolation. Which is hard if you haven't experienced consolation. But remember, they are seasons and like the actual seasons, they are out of your control. Try to believe that if you are in winter there will come a spring, a summer, a turn of the earth.

What if you never get clear guidance on your question? What if none of these approaches yield any felt sense of an answer? You've still participated fully in an intentional decision-making process and that is valuable. Understanding your responsibilities, values and the impacts of your narratives is always helpful, and your decisions will be better because of it. Whatever you choose will be right for you.

I've had very clear discernment processes with all sorts of guidance and the decision still brought difficulties and turned out differently than I hoped. There's no magic wand. Most decisions involve loss, because when we decide to do one thing we are often deciding not to do something else, which can bring grief for you and others. Getting clear guidance doesn't always make a decision easy.

I've also used a discernment process and not received an answer, or any clear felt sense of guidance. The information gathered is still useful if I need to make the decision intellectually. My pros and cons list will be richer and more complete, and I can reconnect and recommit to my values. Knowing you made the most intentional decision possible with the information you had will reassure you that you did the best you could. And you'll get better at it. The next decision, and the one after that, and the one after that will give you a chance to practice, and it will become easier, more natural.

Your Thoughts

Part Five

Resistance and Support

CHAPTER TWENTY-SIX

Navigating Resistance and Embracing Discomfort

Discernment around a life transition or a job decision is a process that takes time. We don't always get all the time we'd like, but ideally, we allow the process to unfold in a way that is organic and unforced. How do you understand the difference between the normal rhythms of learning and resistance? What is helpful resistance and where can it be limiting? What if it hurts? This section looks at ways in which we may run into discomfort, or discover barriers to our discernment. You may have your own, and hopefully you can share them with a trusted friend or in your community to understand how to best honor your own challenges.

Honor resistance

Sometimes we get stuck. The notebook or file in which we are writing about our discernment journey sits untouched for weeks or months. The concepts that initially engaged us seem empty or stupid. You might mean to read this book, but it nevertheless sits untouched on your bedside table for months. You might wonder why you ever thought this would be helpful.

These pauses or slow spaces are a part of most significant undertakings – education, career, marriage, training for a race, any artistic project or spiritual undertaking. It is important to honor the resistance you may encounter and get curious about it.

First, trust yourself. If you find this work to be especially enervating, if even thinking about going to your notebook or space or picking up this book seems like more than you can deal with right now, then put the work aside. Get curious about what might be happening for you. If the concept of trusting that you know what is best for you is relatively novel, trusting that you are right when you think you need a break or rest can be unfamiliar. We have many cultural messages about powering through. We have few messages about listening to ourselves and putting our feet up for a while when we're tired.

Try some of the Jesuit concepts we've discussed. Rest where you find fruit. If a process is helpful, energizing and life-giving, keep doing it. When it stops being life-giving, consider alternatives. This instruction was meant for prayer and contemplation, which is very similar to what we are doing.

The Jesuits also refer to the ups and downs of spiritual life as seasons. When things are great, and you feel connected it's called Consolation. When things are difficult and everything seems dry and lifeless, it's called Desolation. The key point is that, just like the actual seasons, you aren't always in charge of the variations in your spiritual or emotional work. In many religious traditions, if you feel a lack of connection with your God you might be told that you did something to cause that. People might suggest you've sinned, or drifted away from your spiritual path. But in the Jesuit frame of Consolation and Desolation it's not necessarily about individual merit or effort. It's just the season. In Seattle, where I live, it often rains. It is raining right now, even though it is June. I had nothing to do with that. It can be much the same with the seasons of Consolation and Desolation. Sometimes you're good, sometimes you're not. Sometimes you're the windshield, sometimes you're the bug.

Sometimes you look at your partner and wonder why on earth you ever chose them. You may ask yourself if they chew their food that way on purpose to irritate you. At other times you look at that same partner with delight and appreciation, struck as they bathe the children or pull groceries out of the back of the car that you are fortunate to have such a wonderful person in your life.

You may go to your job as a teacher and feel a sense of connection and mission, thinking of all the young people you get to help in your work each day. At another time you may feel nothing but frustration and wonder what on earth you were thinking when you agreed to teach seventh grade this year.

Honor resistance. Sometimes the resistance you feel to a process like this is a way for your deep self to say we need a minute. Give yourself the time. Just as sleep can assist our brains in consolidating information and learnings, rest on our spiritual journey can help our souls consolidate and absorb new ways of being with the Divine. You may need to sit with a concept or idea for a while until you get a sense of its importance in your decision-making process. You may look at one of the chapters of this book and think no way can I deal with that theme right now. Listen to that.

Often, we are told to override our intuitive reactions. "No pain no gain" messages are not helpful when it comes to listening to ourselves in an intentional process of discernment. We are not at the gym. This is not a competition. Be as gentle and compassionate with yourself as you can and honor resistance when it comes up.

Embracing discomfort

Often, when people find out that I believe in God and have a spiritual practice they say that must be nice for me. Often those who don't believe in God assume that believing in God makes everything easier, like having an invisible friend with you all the time, a friend who finds you parking spots.

That's not what it's been like for me. Think of an important relationship you have – with a spouse, or sibling or child. It brings you joy, but it might not always make your life easier or softer. Sometimes the relationship itself can cause you discomfort – the worry about a sister with a drug habit, or an ongoing disagreement with a partner, or all the things you give up to care for a child.

We can grow up with a childish notion that love relationships are always passionate and connected and that those feelings will persist for years. I've known people who ended stable, loving marriages because the "in love" sensation they had at the beginning of the relationship waned after time, or children, or life stresses. People can idealize a relationship with a Higher Power as well. They can think that if an early connection is gone and the dynamic has shifted that the relationship is over or, in the case of a spiritual relationship, never existed at all.

Being on a spiritual path can be uncomfortable. Sometimes we need to acknowledge and embrace that discomfort as part of the path rather than trying to fix it or avoid it. In the Christian tradition, the Holy Spirit came to Jesus and drove him out into the desert for forty days and forty nights. I know that Spirit, the one who says time to leave your friends, be alone, fast, be tempted and tested. Sometimes knowing and getting guidance from your Higher Power means being told you have to go out into your own desert. And that can be acutely uncomfortable.

Looking at my values and making hard calls about what I believe and what that means for my life can be painful. Sitting with my inner community can be difficult. When I have been called to scrutinize old narratives that no longer serve me, I am often unsettled. If I let go of them, I am disoriented and ask myself what do I believe now? Sometimes I miss the old stories and the identities

I used to cling to the way I missed drinking when I first got sober. Each of the pieces of the discernment process can cause discomfort. And if you get a hard answer to the question you are discerning, if you hear something that isn't going to make your life easier or softer, if it's something people you care for will protest, that too can be challenging. If it hurts, it isn't necessarily bad. It might even be badly needed for you to have the kind of authentic life you are looking for. Embrace discomfort where you can, share it with a guide or trusted friend, but don't be surprised if it shows up.

On procrastination

We each have to find the balance between discipline and finding a pace that suits us in whatever our life circumstances are at the time. If you're concerned you are procrastinating rather than experiencing resistance, you might need to try something more structured. Find a way to carve out time for this process. It could be as simple as an alarm on your phone to remind you to spend twenty minutes every Saturday afternoon with this content.

Most of the time I do anything remotely spiritual, it's a slow start. I rarely feel inclined to do whatever I am doing, and often don't feel spiritual while I'm doing it. I like ritual, so I get a cup of tea, light a candle and sometimes set an intention or pray before I start. This can get me over the (many) times when I'm reluctant to get started, or am distracted, or both. I no longer have an expectation that I'm going to feel a certain way, so I'm not surprised or disappointed when prayer, meditation or discernment is about as enlightening and consoling as brushing my teeth. When I started, I wanted my holy to *show*. It turns out, I need to show up to get to the holy.

If you're not sure if you're busy, resisting, or procrastinating, try this. Set a timer for three minutes. Then do this work for three minutes. Read a page. Write a paragraph in your journal. Give yourself permission to stop after three minutes, or to continue. If you find yourself continuing after three minutes, then you may just be procrastinating. You may need a bit more structure to fit this process into your life. But if those three minutes feel like thirty and you leap up as soon as the timer sounds, it might be resistance. You might need a break.

If you are busy, you may find that you make more progress with five minutes a day for a few days a week than an hour every other week. Being exposed to the ideas, reminding your subconscious that you are on a path to greater understanding might be more beneficial in the long run than doing big swathes of work less often. But if you have an intuitive sense that you need a break, honor it. We should listen to the part of us that says not this work right now, or not in this way.

On fear

Last night I woke up at three thirty-three am. My grandkids were spending the night, and Ruby is in a phase where she wakes up at four-thirty in the morning, so I tried hard to get back to sleep. But I couldn't because I was afraid. I was afraid that a decision I was making would turn out badly. It wasn't rational. It wasn't reasonable. It wasn't even connected to the here and now, I was afraid that bad things that had happened to me in the past would happen again. But I was really afraid. Like, blood run cold afraid.

I tried all the things that people suggest when you wake up in the middle of the night. Breathe deeply, meditate, scan your body and relax each muscle group. I did them all but remained wide awake and afraid. How, I thought, am I supposed to discern if my connection to any inner knowing is obscured by fear? Oh, wait, I should put that in the book.

Fear. "This short word somehow touches about every aspect of our lives. It was an evil and corroding thread; the fabric of our existence was shot through with it." (BB p. 67) In the Twelve Steps, the personal inventory in Step Four contains a list of fears. "We reviewed out fears thoroughly. We put them on paper." (BB p. 28)

If fear is impeding your ability to make a decision, then understanding what you are afraid of can be a useful start. Writing down your fears, even the unreasonable ones or the ones that seem silly, can bring clarity, especially if you have a guide or friend you can talk to about your fears. It can be a relief to remember that many of us have fears about the same things; public speaking, spiders, being betrayed or abandoned, being penniless, being alone.

One of my big fears is that the people I love will die young, in a tragic, unexpected way. That's how I lost my father and my son. As I've written elsewhere, death knows my address. My natural tendency to be Worst Case Scenario Girl has been exacerbated by those experiences. Both of those losses were traumatic in different ways. Many years of therapy have given me coping skills and understanding, but the trauma is still in my body, and it can come up again.

If discernment is me trying to listen to a still small voice, fear is like a series of airplanes roaring overhead, obscuring the voice. Then I get panicked on top of the fear because if I can't connect to myself, if I can't get past the fear, how will I know what to do? Where will I find guidance?

Since I believe in a Higher Power, I start there. Bill Wilson suggests we ask our Higher Power to remove our fear. "We ask Him to remove our fear and direct our attention to what He would have us be. At once, we commence to outgrow fear. (BB p. 68)" I don't use the gendered language, but I like the prayer. I've been known to repeat it over and over again in my mind while waiting in the security line at the airport. "At once" means right away, but, to be fair, what we are actually doing is *starting* to outgrow fear. "At once, we commence to outgrow fear" means, to me, we start to begin to outgrow fear. Which can take time. But sometimes this prayer will bring me relief, even if it's just acting as a mantra to quiet my mind.

I will also use my intellect and reason. I can obsess on pretty outlandish fears. Sometimes I'll ask myself what the chances of that thing happening really are? In C.S. Lewis' book *The Screwtape Letters*, he writes from the perspective of a demon who is tempting a man. Essentially, the demon suggests that if we are fixated on fears of what might happen in the future, we can spin multiple scenarios and worry about them all, even if the scenarios would cancel each other out. God gives us fortitude to deal with actual difficulties in our real life, but not the thousand dire scenarios we spin up in our mind. The man who gets a cancer diagnosis and feels terror about his health and mortality is dealing with a present, actual fear, a real difficulty. A man who obsesses about getting cancer in the future, with no rational basis for that concern, may feel acutely uncomfortable, but, according to Lewis, the problem he should solve isn't getting protection from a future cancer, but discovering a way to stay grounded in the present and metabolize his chronic worries about his health. And, of course, we should be alert when fear and anxiety might need to be treated by a therapist or other professional.

My mind will throw up fear to distract me from any number of less admirable emotions, like wanting to be in control, or selfishness or greed. For me, fear is often connected to old grief. See Chapter 28 for more about discerning through grief. When I write down my fears, I try to understand what might be beneath that. If I am worrying obsessively about the welfare of someone I love who is healthy, then it might be a clue that an old grief is arising.

Going back to your Inner Community may be helpful. Who in the inner chamber of your soul is sounding the alarm? Is there any other part of you that could comfort the one who is frightened? Is there anything that comes up in that noise of fear? In my Inner Community, it's always the same part that is shrieking with terror and keeping everyone awake. I know what she looks like and why she sounds the alarms. And I have other parts that I imagine coming to comfort her. Sometimes it helps, sometimes it doesn't, but in the middle of the night it gives me something to think about that isn't the worry itself.

Last night, Ruby came into my room just as I was drifting off. She crawled in bed next to me and cuddled up. I was hoping she would go back to sleep. We were lying on our sides facing each other. Her face was so close to mine that I could feel her breath on my nose. She held my hand and put her little feet on the tops of my legs. I want knowing to be like that, I want my Higher Power to give me guidance like that – in the midst of the fear, in the middle of the noise, to walk up the stairs, climb into bed, cuddle up and cut through the clutter of fear with the undeniable presence of love. Maybe at the wrong time, maybe in a way that's inconvenient, maybe as a small voice when I want something big and dramatic. But real.

Your Thoughts

CHAPTER TWENTY-SEVEN

When being in the body hurts

The Spiritual Exercises of Ignatius of Loyola started with a wound. Ignatius broke his leg, and the healing was painful and arduous. While he was healing, he started using imagination and contemplation, paying specific attention to how his reactions showed up in his physical being. He suggests using our imagination and concentrating on our sense experiences, taste, smell, sight, touch, hearing. This is an approach that focuses on the body and the wisdom in our bodies. It can be hard to listen to our bodies. Trauma, physical pain or illness, grief and loss can all make tuning into our bodies painful and difficult.

I always appreciate it when a leader or facilitator says to a group "anyone who is able . . ." when asking people to do a physical action, like stand or walk. This whole book is "as you are able." Which means honoring the wounded places in our bodies or spirits that make it a challenge to sit, meditate or even connect with our bodies.

I have chronic pain in my hips. When it's bad, I find myself dissociating from my body. I walk around as if I am a brain on a stick. The stick is my body, but I pay as little attention to it as possible because tuning into that channel means acknowledging the pain. I can tune out the pain, but then I'm also tuning out all the good things that come in my body. One of the reasons I meditate in the morning rather than the evening, is that by the evening it feels too threatening to sink down into the embodied experience of the day. Physical as well as emotional pain can make it difficult to tune into our bodies. And I think we should honor that resistance if needed.

After my son died, I had terrific anxiety for years. The trauma of his injury and death lodged in my body and I could feel it when I exercised. I love to swim. I appreciate the liminal space created when I'm moving through the water. It doesn't feel like other exercise – it's more like meditation. The rhythmic nature of the movement increases the meditative action; it is ancient, the crawling movement, my head turning left and right to sip the air between strokes.

At the time I was working in downtown Seattle, near the YMCA. I would walk up to the Y on my lunch break and change in the women's locker room and take an elevator to the basement where the pool was. It's an old building, and it was an old elevator. I don't like elevators or closed spaces under the best of circumstances, but wearing just a bathing suit and flip flops made it much worse. The pool wasn't usually crowded, and once I was in the water, I enjoyed the movement, and it calmed me. But then I finished swimming and had to return to the elevator, toweling dry, still damp and in a bathing suit and flip flops. We have earthquakes in Seattle occasionally and I would think about the Big One happening while I was in a steel trap in an old brick building. Seattle was built on a void, built over another older city by filling in the spaces with garbage. I'd try to remember the map in my head, was the YMCA over that old underground Seattle? By the time I was in the shower, my breathing would be shallow, and I'd feel lightheaded. I'd become convinced that I would faint, that a stranger would find me laid out on the old tile, unconscious and naked. It wasn't until I called my friend Juliette that she asked the helpful question. "Have you ever passed out in the shower at the Y?"

"No," I answered.

"Have you ever passed out anywhere?"

"No. I mean, I passed out after Emma was born, directly after I delivered her. But other than that, no."

"So why do you think you're going to now pass out in the shower at the Y?"

I had no answer for that. It was, of course, one of those distortions anxiety can create. But when I got nervous in the shower, I would remember Juliette's question, and concentrate on the fact I had never passed out in the shower and tell myself this was just anxiety, not actually a sign that I was going to lose consciousness.

I realized later that I carry grief in my hips, which makes sense. I gave birth to RJ, I carried him as a baby on my hips. I lifted him in and out of his wheelchair after his brain injury, using my hips as a fulcrum. Something about swimming loosens whatever is in my hips and it comes into my awareness in a different way, which can be frightening. I can't titrate my body's release of emotions, so I was scared it would be too much, it would overwhelm me, that I would have a violent reaction like vomiting or fainting or convulsing. Never mind that none of those things had ever happened because of a strong emotion coming out of my body. Usually, I just cried for a bit and then felt better. But I had spent so much time being vigilant about keeping difficult emotions suppressed or just walled off that it scared me.

Finally, I stopped swimming. I loved the exercise, but the rest of the experience was too much for me. I honored that resistance. I went to therapy and learned about somatic experiencing and the impact of trauma on the body. But it still took years until I was ready to swim again. When I returned to swimming, I went to a pool that was on the ground floor and involved no elevators. I had my daughter come with me the first few times, and her presence in the next lane, the even motion of her arms, soothed me.

The channel of your body may not be the best channel for you. That might be temporary, or it might last longer. That may be the resistance you need to honor in this process. The dominant culture is very definitive about which bodies "belong" and are "acceptable" and which are not. And it is generally cruel to bodies who don't fit into the narrow confines of what is socially acceptable. After my son was in a car accident, he spent the rest of his life in a wheelchair. If we were out in public, people would look through him, or look away, erasing his body, his existence. Any kind of travel, even in a car to my Aunt Tanya's house, was difficult. Air travel was horrendous.

When I look at my granddaughter, her little legs, her hands, I see the comfort and ease she has being in her body. No one has told her there is anything wrong with her body, with her. It makes me sad that so many of us don't get to keep that. Some of us don't even start with that, the messages of wrongness begin when we're infants. I hope that her journey through the world in her strong female body is better and safer than mine was.

If traditional ways of listening to the wisdom of the body are not readily available to us, I believe that our deepest understanding will find a way to make herself known. You might find that the other ways of knowing, like attraction and aversion, or intuitive thoughts may be ascendant. Your dream life or imagination may become especially active. Find what channel is best for you.

When I was dealing with the way my body processed the loss of my son, my spiritual director suggested that when physical or emotional pain or discomfort comes up in my body, I should find where in my body the pain is most acute and place the palm of my hand on that place. Welcome the sensation and be curious about what it might be telling me – without judgement or any thought of controlling it. I find it hard to do that, but even the intention of doing that eases my discomfort. Breathe. Keep breathing. This will pass.

Thomas Keating, the Trappist monk who reintroduced Centering Prayer to Christians, suggested this prayer in response to any emotion or sensation. Here's the entire prayer, but I often shorten it to just "Welcome."

Welcome, welcome, welcome. I welcome everything that comes to me today because I know it's for my healing. I welcome all thoughts, feelings, emotions, persons, situations, and conditions. I let go of my desire for power and control. I let go of my desire for affection, esteem, approval, and pleasure. I let go of my desire for survival and security. I let go of my desire to change any situation, condition, person or myself. I open to the love and presence of God and God's action within. Amen.

This prayer also offers a useful checklist for me. Often, if I am resisting an emotion, sensation or experience, it's because I'm trying to control it. My "desire for affection, esteem and approval" causes me to worry about what other people will think if I am vulnerable. My desire for security can manifest as wanting my own way, trying to manipulate another person or situation. Each of these are age old human tricks to push away the truth, the spiritual core, or the essence of our experience. These human tricks can show up and pretend to be resistance I should honor, but really, it's just self-will in disguise.

When difficult emotions or sensations crowd in, I try to believe they might be for my healing. I don't, as Keating writes "know it's for my healing." I don't have that kind of faith yet. But to even hold out the possibility, to consider that this might be for my healing in a way I don't yet understand, is helpful.

I believe that everything that exists is sacramental, it is imbued with Spirit and therefore good and holy. That includes my body and your body. The word "namaste" means that my spirit salutes the spirit within you. What if we, as a society, as individuals, acted as if our bodies were sacred? What if we saluted the bodies that carry us through the world? Not just my body, or the bodies of my friends, but the bodies of drug addicts, the incarcerated, the elderly and infirm?

Recovering alcoholics sometimes use something called the "set aside prayer", asking that they may arrive at a new way of thinking about alcoholism and God. I find this to be a useful prayer for me to re-envision my relationship with my body as well. Here's my adaptation, which you can address to whomever you address your prayers or intentions.

Help me set aside everything I think I know about you, myself, and my body, so that I may have a new experience and a new understanding of you, myself, and my body.

Since one of my "inordinate attachments" is to the stories I've told myself and my beliefs about the world, any version of the "set aside prayer" can help me recognize that the stories, my beliefs and my understanding are mutable, they can be set aside. I can set aside things I think I know about my body or my pain and be open to a new experience and a new understanding.

Your Thoughts

CHAPTER TWENTY-EIGHT

Grief and Loss

People often say that you shouldn't make any major decisions after a loss or bereavement. When I got sober people told me not to make any big changes in my life in the first year. For one thing, just staying sober was going to take lots of focus and energy, so I didn't need to be distracted by changes. Also, as I was learning to live without alcohol, I might not be in the best frame of mind to make decisions about my life.

But, soon after I got sober, my husband, the father of my two children, asked for a divorce. Life happens. You can't always insulate yourself from changes or difficulties when you are processing a loss. After my son died, I was in quite a bit of debt from his medical bills, so I felt I had to return to work quickly. I had another teenager to take care of, I had other obligations.

Our culture isn't very understanding about how long grief takes. I always felt like there was a very short timeline and I was exceeding it in my profligate grief over my son's death. But at least people understood the loss of a child. Other griefs that loom large for us can be discounted or ignored by our families, communities, or the culture at large. The loss of a job or a career, the loss of health or youth or physical ability, the loss of financial security, the loss of a romantic relationship or a friendship, the end of a marriage, the death of a pet; any of these losses can be devastating even if they are dismissed or discounted by others.

If you have experienced recent loss or grief and are discerning a significant life change, it may be helpful to wait to make a decision. But you may not have that luxury or option. I found grief to be so overwhelming it was hard to see or hear anything else internally. The signposts I used to understand what I wanted to do were obscured. Discerning my spiritual direction using attraction or aversion, connecting to my body, using my imagination – all of those avenues were very difficult to connect with. I could still do discernment, I just needed to lean more heavily into the other avenues available to me.

The tool that was useful to me when I was grieving was intuitive thought that came from a strong sense of spiritual connection. For all my anger at God for the death of my son, I was in a long period of spiritual consolation after he died. I felt like the Divine was very close and offering support. Praying through anger at God was something I learned years ago when my father died.

I was nineteen when my father died and still developing my adult spiritual beliefs. I knew I didn't believe in a God who pulls all the strings and arranges everything, because then we wouldn't have free will, which is important. My father died from a rare heart disease. I knew that. But I wanted a different God, I wanted a God who kept my father alive longer. My family prayed for my father; our large extended family prayed for him. He wore a scapular, a piece of cloth with religious significance. They are known by their color; Catholics refer to the Brown Scapular or the Green Scapular. My father wore the green one, a devotion to Mary. It's a small piece of green cloth that you wear around your neck, it hangs from thin strips of felt-like cloth. Some of them have a square of cloth in the front and in the back. I wore one once, I bought the one that has multiple scapulars together, each scapular with a color, all the colors bound together like a tiny colored children's book, one copy hanging between my breasts, another in the middle of my back. Of course, these are blessed by a priest. And still he died. He probably died with that scapular around his neck. I wonder if the paramedics ripped it off when they were trying to get his heart to start again.

I got sober when I was twenty-six, a little over six years after my father's death. And in early sobriety all the grief and rage and ragged emotional baggage I had been carrying and drinking to keep hidden spilled out all over me. I went to talk with a Catholic priest. I told him I was having trouble praying. He asked me why. I told him that I was mad at God because my father had died so young.

"Talk to God just like you're talking to me," he said. He was my parish priest. I don't remember his name, but looking back now I realize he was young, probably in his thirties. He was quiet and calm, small in stature.

"But I can't," I said.

"Why not?

"Because I'm so angry I would cuss. I would cuss at God."

He looked at me kindly. "That's ok. You can cuss. You can cuss at God."

I don't know how long it took me to actually do that, but when I did pray, I brought my anger. I was mad at God. Mad that my husband had left me, angry that I had to stop drinking and now deal with the waves of grief and emotion that were rising up without the anesthetic of alcohol. But I also longed for a connection to God. I believed in a God. I just didn't believe in a God who was interested in me or involved in my life in any way.

I looked up at the ceiling and prayed. My first words were "fuck you." I said fuck you to God. I waited for a minute, half expecting a lightning bolt to strike me. Nothing happened so I started telling God what I was angry about, and in a few minutes, I was weeping. I cried so hard I had to sit down on the floor. I felt this strong sense of connection, and a relief that the priest had been right, it was as easy as talking to God, cuss words and all. I now call this the 'Fuck You prayer' and recommend it highly to my friends. It's not the colloquy Ignatius imagined, but it worked for me. You're welcome to try it.

Grief and loss can be the start of a conversion experience. Or it can push people away from any spiritual practice or community, especially when a community is unskillful. I think particularly of people who say that the dead loved one is "with God" or "in a better place," or that their death was "God's will" as phrases tailor-made to drive people away from a spiritual connection or the community that uses those phrases. But for many, the loss makes an opening for new or reclaimed belief and spiritual connection.

> "*Both the Spiritual Exercises and Alcoholics Anonymous assume that conversion begins with a deep sense of human brokenness.*" (Harbaugh p.xv)

I have found this to be true. A deep sense of our human brokenness doesn't have to be just about our personal brokenness, the way alcoholics understand fully that they are alcoholics when they "hit bottom" and experience damaging consequences from their drinking. It can be recognizing the deep sense of the brokenness of our human nature or human systems. RJ died because the medical system in the United States is more about making a profit than caring for patients. I have a deep sense of the human brokenness that results from capitalism, white supremacy, rapacious greed, and exploitation of human beings and nature. That can be the starting point for a conversion, although I often don't recognize it until I look back.

If you are making a decision while you're in grief or after a recent loss, here are suggestions that I found to be helpful.

- Seek out the counsel of a trusted friend or advisor. While we can all use this, I found this to be especially helpful when I was trying to make decisions in grief. Make sure your friend or advisor doesn't have a vested interest in the decision you are making, or has the emotional maturity to put that aside. What do they think? Is that helpful to you?

- If you are angry with your Higher Power be careful about who you share that with and make sure you are talking to someone who, like the priest I consulted, can understand and accept that anger towards the Divine can be part of our relationship with the Divine. No one would be surprised if someone expressed anger at their spouse or parent. But I've had people get really judgmental when I talk about being angry with God. I have a relationship with God. And sometimes God pisses me off. People can become very uncomfortable with that concept. "Rightly and naturally, we think well before we choose the person or persons with who to take this intimate and confidential step." (BB p.74) That's in reference to finding the person who will hear the personal inventory written in Step Four, which happens in Step Five. But it's useful in looking for a person to speak with about your spiritual path through grief and loss as well, or any spiritual director or advisor.

- Work with a therapist or counselor. I started back to therapy soon after RJ died, and it was very helpful with both the grieving process and with understanding all the other trauma that was coming up. I always describe grief like folding chairs shoved in a closet. When I open the closet to add another chair, another grief, sometimes the old chairs or losses fall out on my head. It was invaluable to have a trained professional to talk with about what came up for me. This also helped me in discernment, since I was able to really dig into the old narratives I was still carrying around.

- If any spiritual practice is helpful or comforting to you, use it. Meditation, attendance at any worship service, even if you no longer believe in it, time in the outdoors, spiritual music – anything that can connect you to the Divine can work.

And if you do have to make a life decision while you're in a season of grief, don't worry. If you have clearly mapped your value system, considered your responsibilities and any limitations, and you've taken counsel from trusted advisors, you can move ahead with confidence that you did the best, most intentional discernment available to you.

Your Thoughts

CHAPTER TWENTY-NINE

Community

A few years after my son RJ died, I realized I had become isolated. I was self-conscious that I was so emotionally wrecked even years after his death, so I pulled back from my wider circle of friends. I am fortunate to have a group of close, long-time friends. But my friends are not connected to one another. In fact, the only time they've all been together was at my daughter's wedding. Most of the time my friends are scattered in various states, and we don't get to see each other in person very often.

After RJ's death, I realized that I needed community. I needed a group of people, a society. Looking back, I realized it was part of my own spiritual discernment process, that inner prompting. I'm deeply introverted, and quite shy, so finding community was daunting.

At first, I tried church. I was a Catholic then, and Catholics are notoriously ineffective at building church communities. There are exceptions, of course, but most can't get past the coffee hour after Mass on Sundays. I kept looking.

I was in graduate school when I met Alexandra. She was the professor for a couple of my classes. She speaks multiple languages and has multiple PhDs. In class, she spoke about spirituality in a way that resonated for me. She is also a nun, a member of the Congregation of St Joseph of Peace. I went to retreats at their space in Bellevue. At the first one I attended, we walked into the small chapel that looks out over Lake Washington. I was uncomfortable with all these strangers. I caught the eye of one of the nuns as I walked in. Most of the nuns are older, many of them in their eighties and nineties. The nun who looked at me had an expression that conveyed that she saw me. She recognized me. I've seen that look before, but only on the face of someone who loved me and knew me well. But she was a stranger. Yet in one look she showed me she understood me and that I was in the right place. She had a deeply mischievous look in her eye, it was welcoming and playful and subversive. I've never had an experience like that before or since, I don't even know her name, but it was profound. I felt a sense of coming home.

These nuns represent a different kind of Catholicism, one that focuses on radical hospitality and social justice. To me, they are all a bunch of radical feminists. They told me that in addition to nuns, or "vowed religious" as they call themselves, they had associates. I became an associate. Associates are lay people who want to participate in the "charism" – what the community is called to do and be in the world. The men and women who join as associates all do different kinds of social justice work, but we support one another in that work wherever it may take us. I went through a discernment process and became an associate.

As an associate I consider myself to be nun adjacent. I didn't take the same vows the nuns take, but I did "covenant" about what I was going to do in the world. I stood up in front of the community and announced the result of my discernment process and felt their support. I find this community very nourishing. I fit in here for the same reasons I don't fit in many other places; I'm curious, iconoclastic, smart, rebellious and spiritual. When I have spoken my truth at work, it's gotten me in trouble. When I speak my truth in community, even if others disagree, there's support for it and a kind of pleasure, as if while we disagree, we are also relishing the fact that we are connected in a way that is not threatened by disagreement.

Most religious communities have associates, although they might be called by another name. Some communities of associates play a more active role than others – our order involves associates deeply. Being nun adjacent felt weird at first, and it took a few years for me to settle into it. I am used to more transactional group dynamics, grounded in capitalism, work, and exploitation. This community is so removed from those ways of being that I was disoriented at first. "Welcome" is so much larger here, so much more generous and generative.

Around this time, in my early fifties, I became an Episcopalian. My friend Alissa from graduate school had become a priest, and she invited me to her new parish south of Seattle. It is in a large round building with a skylight in the center of the roof from which sunlight shines down on the altar.

I felt at home there also, from the moment I walked in. I felt it in my body. It was so different from the Catholic Churches I once attended. The parish has many young children, and before they go off to their Sunday school, which is called Godly Play, they play with the toys stacked in bins at the back of the church; dolls and building blocks. The community is diverse, and on Pentecost, people read the selected texts in their native language, which might be French or Arabic or Spanish, while I read the English version in the handout. The neighborhood is not a wealthy area. We have a community garden in the back of the church for members of the refugee community to grow vegetables. There's a food bank, and beehives.

Alissa is a master at building community, and I went along. I joined groups and took classes and built relationships over time. Ruby goes to church with me most Sundays, and sits at my feet on the play rugs playing with toys. Ruby likes to run, and when we get to church early, she will do a few laps around the church. She'll run past the altar, down an aisle, behind the chairs on the side, past the baptismal font, and then around the altar again, waving and smiling to me as she passes. She runs steadily, with purpose, and it is pretty adorable. Older members of the community who also get to church early exchange glances with me. We do that with each other, share a smile when one of the young toddlers dances to the music, or distributes holy water with a generous wave of a branch that splashes us in the face. I love that Ruby is growing up in a community that celebrates however she chooses to express herself.

Getting started in community was challenging since I was used to a transactional way of interacting with groups, where success was based on conformity and productivity. I had to relearn and let go of many narratives about who I was and how I was allowed to show up. Introverts can be part of community. You can be welcomed as you are, without demands to produce or work or add value.

Being in community can be difficult. That's part of the spiritual discipline of it, and where there are opportunities for growth. People disagree. We must find ways to navigate differences and repair ruptures. We can't leave racism and other social evils at the door when we enter, we have to encounter and navigate those in community as well. And we have to show up. Meeting after meeting, service after service, month after month, year after year.

Americans aren't good at community anymore. In May of 2023 the US Surgeon General Dr. Vivek Murthy issued an advisory on the dangerous epidemic of loneliness and isolation in the United States. We're lonelier and more isolated than ever, and it's damaging our mental health and physical well-being. Community is good for our mental health as well as our spiritual health. But how can we find community?

If you are part of a religious tradition, it might be easier. Both of my communities are connected with a faith tradition. Shop around. Attend different gatherings. Pay attention to cues you get from your body, any attraction or aversion that arises. In both of my communities I knew I was in the right place because I felt an intense attraction and sense of belonging. I was right. But they both, objectively, align with my values. I once attended a beautiful church service with a friend whose daughter was singing in the choir. I was attracted to the worship service, and could see that the community was home to my friend's daughter. Then she started telling me that homosexuality was a sin, a fast-train-to-hell sin. "But we love the sinner, even if we hate the sins." Not my kind of community because their beliefs don't align with my values.

If you are not part of a faith tradition, you could consider any intentional community. It might be a group of people who connect to work on something that they believe needs to change in the world. It may be a group that helps unhoused teens or one that gathers to keep invasive plants out of the forests. Different people from various walks of life gather to help. Reciprocity works in groups. If a group is trying to help the world in some way, the world will help back.

Any group that gathers in kindness or intention can become community, from a hiking group to open water swimmers to knitters to a book club. All groups have group agreements, whether they are explicit or not. Here are signs of a healthy community to look for when you are searching:

- Power is shared. There isn't one person who is the only leader, or the only authority. Formal leadership should change often, and informal leaders should be generous, kind, and open to different views.
- Conflict and differences of opinion are tolerated, and people treat one another kindly, or at least politely, even when they differ. Tempers may flare, but after the argument, are the people who disagreed kind or polite to each other? Is there a process or guidelines for having tough conversations, either explicit or culturally understood?
- New members are welcomed and oriented in some way. The orientation is more "here's where the bathrooms are and every third Sunday we go out to pizza and everyone chips in for it" and less "you have to believe and do and buy what we do to belong." The ideal here is radical hospitality.
- Ideally, communities have no entrance fees or financial motives. Expenses are shared, with accommodations to help those with less ability to pay.

During the pandemic, many groups moved to a virtual format and gathered online. Virtual connections can be lovely – I'm always happy to see the nuns in our community who live in England and New Jersey when we have online gatherings. But meeting in person does help to build the interconnectedness more efficiently. Because we are wired to be in community, our bodies recognize and reinforce community connections – we feel closer to people with whom we do any exercise, for example. A virtual community is better than no community, but it's great to have opportunities to meet in person and build those connections in a different, embodied way. If only so you can secretly marvel at who turns out to be taller or shorter in person than you thought they'd be when you saw them online.

Finally, you can also build community yourself. You could gather a group of people to go through this book, or other books like this in an intentional book club of your own design. During the pandemic when our church was closed, the vicars set up small groups to meet online. I was not interested, and thought it was a dumb idea, but I went along because a couple of my friends were in the group. To my surprise, the six of us became very close, and the closeness has continued now that we can meet in person.

If you're going to set up a group yourself, be clear about group agreements, and spend time together determining them. For example, do you want everything shared in the group to be confidential? How often should you meet? What is the structure and format? Are there any services needed, like finding a place to meet or bringing beverages or cleaning up? How can you rotate service positions? How do you handle conflict? Are there any communication guidelines; can people talk more than once before everyone has spoken? Is there a time limit on how long people can talk? Can you give advice to one another or not? How do you feel about cussing? Interrupting? Punctuality to start and end the meeting? Consider the guidelines for healthy groups, above, but each group can decide what works best for the people in it.

The next chapter describes a specific discernment process that can be done in community, and might be a way to both get guidance and build community, if that appeals to you.

Your Thoughts

CHAPTER THIRTY

Clearness Committee

My friend James was discerning if he wanted to become an Episcopal priest. Since I was beginning to develop the content of this book, and thinking about different discernment models, I was interested in his process for discernment.

The diocese of Olympia in Washington State, where we live, has a process for vocational discernment for people who are considering ordination. It takes a number of years. One part of the process is to gather a group from your community to help with discernment. I was part of James' group. There were six of us and James. One member was a retired priest from another parish, but the rest of us all go to church together and know one another. We are different ages, genders, and races, but we all agreed to spend a year meeting with James to help him discern.

We went through a specific set of topics provided by the Diocese in each of our monthly meetings. Because it was at the end of the pandemic, we met remotely. A year of meetings seemed daunting when we started. I thought I'd get more information about this particular process of discernment, but I didn't think I'd get much more out of it myself, although I was happy to help my friend. I was mistaken. Over a year, as I considered each of the questions that James was reviewing, I, too, would learn more about my assumptions around, say, authority or power. In listening to the thoughts of the other members of the group I would often reconsider or expand my understanding. It was deeply fruitful and at the end of the year I was sorry to leave.

The idea of community helping in discernment isn't a new one. And I also don't think it has to be limited to people who are in a religious community together, as we are with James. I like the model of a clearness committee, which I first did in graduate school. A clearness committee comes from the Quaker tradition. It's similar to what we did with James, only with less structure and a shorter time commitment.

Basically, a group of people who know you and care for you gather to help you understand more about your decision. They don't give advice, they don't tell you what to do, they don't talk about their own experience. What they do is ask skillful questions to clear away anything that is blocking you from your own understanding of what it is that is best for you.

The Quakers are also known as the Society of Friends. The Jesuits are also known as the Society of Jesus. Community is in the name. The Quakers, like the Jesuits, believe that each of us has access to an Inner Wisdom. We don't need priests or ministers or intermediaries to tell us what that Inner Wisdom is guiding us to do, or understand or be, we just need to learn how to access that knowing. We can help one another do this in community, in our chosen society.

Is a clearness committee right for you and your discernment process? See if you're attracted to the idea as you read through this chapter. Imagine yourself sitting comfortably in a room with friends as they ask you questions about your situation to help you gain understanding. Does that attract you or repel you? Do you have people who come to mind? Are you in a community or family where people would be open to this exploration and could be helpful? Are you in the habit of asking people for advice?

I come from an Italian family where there is a Padrone, my Uncle Carl, and he is not shy about chiming in with advice, help or guidance, so for me to ask my elders for help with decisions was something I grew up with, and have always done. Other families may not be helpful, or may be insistent that you hew to certain values or paths and could harm a discernment process. Or you may not be situated where you have people you would trust with this, or with whom you can share this process.

You could also do a series of clearness committees. I know of a group in which each session was a clearness committee discernment process for one of the members of the group and they rotated through the group so everyone that wanted to was able to have a session focused on their question or issue.

If you do decide to do a clearness committee, here is a guide. Of course, adapt it to your circumstances or the promptings of your own Inner Wisdom. Note that a clearness committee is usually called and coordinated by the person who is asking the question, who I will call the Seeker. You can suggest a clearness committee for another person, or let them know that it exists, but it's up to the person asking the question or deciding a direction to ask for this help.

Instructions for a Clearness Committee

1. Seeker, pick your people, your Listeners. Ideally, you have four or five, but one or two people can work. It is better to have a few people who can

understand what you are doing and support you than more who might not be suited to this practice.

2. Make sure they understand what they are being asked to do. You could have them read this chapter or find resources from the Quaker tradition with more specific instructions. You are inviting them to participate in a group session where they will ask you questions to help you gain clarity on the decision you are making. The actual meeting itself should be at least an hour, and no longer than two hours. You can do this in one session. You can always add another session if that seems helpful. While our group with James met on video because it was during the pandemic, it is preferable to meet in person if you can, although if video is the only way to do it, that can work. However you meet, make sure to limit distractions. Keep phones off, no multitasking, choose a time and place where you won't be interrupted.
3. The Seeker should write out the specific issue on which they want clarity. They should include any details that are germane. Using the process I've outlined so far in this book, for example, you would include the question you are discerning and any practical obligations you have. This should be brief, no more than a page, and can be sent to the committee in advance so they can sit with it for a while, at least a day or two.
4. At the beginning of the meeting, spend no more than 10 minutes deciding on group agreements, or how you will orient as a group. Start with a moment of quiet to center yourselves. Here is a sample list of Group Agreements, although they may be adapted.
    - We will keep everything that is said here in confidence.
    - We, the Listeners, will only ask questions. The point of these questions is not to satisfy our curiosity but to help the Seeker better understand their situation.
    - We, the Listeners will not offer opinions, advice, commentary or stories of our experiences or the experience of anyone else.
    - We will allow silence and quiet as it arises.
    - Everyone will have a chance to ask questions, and no one speaker on the committee will dominate.
    - The Seeker will be given time and space to consider and thoughtfully answer each question in turn. The Seeker can decline to answer any question at any time and does not have to offer a reason.

Review these group agreements and see if anyone has anything else to add, or if any of these need to be adapted.

5. Choose one person to be the Timekeeper. They can lead the group agreements discussion and the closing questions. If someone forgets the group agreements or begins to give advice rather than asking questions, anyone can offer a gentle reminder of the group agreements, but the Timekeeper should be the one specifically tasked with keeping the gathering on track with the group agreements. The Timekeeper can open the meeting with a moment of quiet either before or after the Group Agreements exercise. If you and your committee share an intention or faith tradition, you can certainly reference that. You may choose to light a candle or play music at the beginning and end to symbolically mark your time together.
6. Towards the end of the meeting, with 15-20 minutes remaining, sit for a few minutes in quiet. Then the Timekeeper can ask the Seeker how they would like to spend the last period of time. Some options are
   - Have a general period of silence for five minutes while the Listeners focus their internal attention on the Seeker. Then any of the Listeners can offer up any observations or images that come up for them as they meditate on the Seeker, always keeping in mind that they are not to offer advice. Think of this as a very short Quaker meeting. A sample observation might be "I hear your deep desire to explore your creativity."
   - The Seeker can ask questions of the Listeners. For example, "Is there anything you are hearing in my discussion of this matter that I don't seem to be aware of? Do I have a blind spot?"
   - The Seeker can ask for appreciation from the Listeners, who can list the strengths and positive attributes and experiences they see in the Seeker that will help them along their way.

Note that many of us are socialized to believe that the best way we can help another is to offer advice, suggestions or instruction. We can talk too much when we get nervous. Or we might insist on centering our own experience. If you are asked to be a Listener, be clear that this is a different space, and you need to truly focus just on asking questions that you think will help the Seeker. For those of us with lots of privilege who tend to give advice freely, this can be challenging.

If you're a Listener, here are examples of potentially helpful questions, assuming the discernment question is about a career, education or job choice.

- Is there anything from your childhood or youth that points to your preference for this kind of work?

- What was your favorite job ever, and what specifically did you appreciate about it?
- Is there anything you fear about making this decision, one way or the other?

Less helpful comments that you will want to avoid are

- When I was your age, I couldn't decide between these two scenarios, and I . . . ."
- Aren't you worried that you won't have enough money for retirement? Do you realize how many women are in financial trouble in their older years?
- There's a book you should read . . . (or podcast you should listen to, etc. etc.)
- You should . . . you need to . . . .

If you're interested in building community, a clearness committee can be a great way to do that. A discernment group, especially one that rotates so each member gets a turn as Seeker, can be a great way to form connections with others. Being a Seeker and then being a Listener can provide growth and new perspectives.

Your Thoughts

CHAPTER THIRTY-ONE

Time and time again

Most significant discernment processes take time. We're not, as a culture, used to things taking time. Generally, we want things quickly. Discernment is slow. How can you stay committed to and accountable for your discernment?

You know best what kind of accountability tools will work for you. But it is good to figure out a way to stay committed to this process when you are in the early stages, when you're enthusiastic and engaged. Because that will pass. And you'll find this book, or see the sticky notes up on the wall at some point in the future and think, oh yeah, that thing. That discernment thing.

For me, discernment is more of a spiritual practice than a decision-making process. And I've learned to wait in spiritual practice without expectations. By thinking of discernment as a spiritual practice, I invite us to consider that it's not going to match our timeline. Our expectations might need to be adjusted or jettisoned altogether. It's a process, yes, but it's more like gardening than building a barn. You plant seeds, you water, you tend and then in due time the plants appear. Or they don't. They produce fruit, although it might not be as much as you expected. Or you might have an unexpected bounty. Last summer I planted raspberries, and this summer they took off, bearing more fruit that I would have thought possible from the small, raised bed. We understand that with gardening or farming, some things are out of our hands. We need to consider nature, the seasons, the vicissitudes of weather and climate and storm. It's the same with discernment. You may not feel like anything is happening, but there might be progress beneath the surface, a marination or germination that is vital but buried.

I'm in Bellevue again today as I write this, with the nuns. I'm in community. I took a break to have lunch with friends, nuns and others. We talked about Ada Limón, the Poet Laureate, and how poetry can clarify and honor. And we laughed, with the laughter that is mainly fueled by a happiness in being together, at that moment.

Poetry sees the significant and elemental in the quotidian. The Catholic tradition believes everything is sacramental, and I share that belief; the bowl of

Cheerios you share with your child, the drive to early morning swim practice, the walk with your dog in the rain, a bubble bath, sex with your wife, the carpenter finishing a cabinet. They can all be holy.

In much the same way, everything can contribute to your discernment. Anything can be rich with meaning for you if you are tuned to that, if you are curious, and ready, and think that it might come.

C.S. Lewis was an atheist before he became a Christian. He wrote that he trusted the word of people who had traveled before him, he trusted the authority of their experience. "I believe there is such a place as New York. I have not seen it myself. I could not prove by abstract reasoning that there must be such a place. I believe it because reliable people have told me so." [1]

Reliable people have listened to the teachings of this Saint and this Drunk and followed their suggestions and changed their lives. Alcoholics and addicts got sober and changed their lives. People turned to the Spiritual Exercises for guidance, direction and strength and got it and it changed their life.

The process will be different for every person. Your journey is unique. But I will tell you that for many of us, the result of the process of discernment can be an answer to our question that arrives with a deep conviction, a soulful, resonant knowing. For me it can be as clear and recognizable as the ringing of a bell. This. This is the way, the choice, the direction, the answer. And I know it to be true by how it sounds, how it feels, the deep resonance inside of me. I can look back on decisions that I've made using discernment and even if it turned out differently than I hoped, or I need to make another discernment later about the same situation, I remember the clarity of that answer and I have confidence that I made the right choice. It might not be right for everyone. Other people may not agree. But I know it's right for me, and that conviction is a relief.

This process can take you there. Over and over again. And the more you do it, the better you'll get at it, and the more you will come to rely on it. Blessings and grace on your journey.

[1] Mere Christianity, C.S. Lewis

Acknowledgements

Thank you to the Congregation of the Sisters of St. Joseph of Peace, who gave me time and space to write this book, especially Alexandra Kovats CSJP, Susan Francois CSJP and Jan Linley, who first suggested the project and helped throughout.

I appreciate the input from the many clients and friends who went through this content with me, especially Ruby Robinson and Caroline Maxwell. Thanks to all who read the book as a work in progress, especially Helen Bell whose belief in what I was doing sustained me.

Thank you to Mirella Lombardo and Kate Mayfield of Shepheard-Walwyn Publishers who picked this book out of the slush pile and decided to help bring it into the world.

And most of all, thanks to my husband, Marcos Martinez, who supported me every step of the way.

Useful books

These books influenced this work, and I invite you to read them if you want to explore some of the following concepts further.

Capitalism and Rest

Rest Is Resistance A Manifesto by Tricia Hersey

12th Step Spirituality

Breathing Under Water Spirituality and the 12 Steps by Richard Rohr OFM

One Breath at a Time: Buddhism and the Twelve Steps by Kevin Griffin

Divine Therapy & Addiction Centering Prayer and the Twelve Steps by Thomas Keating

12-Step Approach to the Spiritual Exercises of St. Ignatius by Jim Harbaugh, S.J.

Spiritual Practice

Everyday Holiness The Jewish Path of Mussar by Alan Morinus

Values

The Live Your Values Deck by Lisa Congdon and Andreea Niculescu

Discernment

A Hidden Wholeness: The Journey Toward An Undivided Life, Welcoming the Soul and Weaving Community in a Wounded World by Parker J. Palmer

Faith: Trusting Your Own Deepest Experience by Sharon Salzberg

The Dark Night of the Soul

Dark Night of the Soul by St. John of the Cross

The Dark Night of the Soul: A Psychiatrist Explores the Connection Between Darkness and Spiritual Growth by Gerald G May

Dark Nights of the Soul: A Guide to Finding Your Way through Life's Ordeals by Thomas Moore

Grief and Loss

The Jewish Way in Death and Mourning by Maurice Lamm

The Wild Edge of Sorrow, Rituals of Renewal and the Sacred Work of Grief by Francis Weller

A Grief Observed by C.S. Lewis

When Things Fall Apart Heart Advice for Difficult Times by Pema Chödrön